# A MOST UNUSUA
## BY
## ANDY KELSO

Hope you enjoy it!

Andy Kelso

# A MOST UNUSUAL JOURNEY

*by*

*Andy Kelso*

**With contributions from:**
**Charm Kelso**
**Brandon, Barney, Tammy, Kim and Beth Kelso**

Published in Great Britain by **Grafted**

www.graftedbydesign.co.uk

ISBN 978-0-9562603-1-4

# Contents:

# ACKNOWLEDGEMENTS

I am deeply grateful to my dear friend Joan for making sense of the manuscript for the printers and for Phil and Cathy for the cover design and printing. I am so grateful to Karen at Worcester Warriors who gave me a computer when ours died and for the enormous help that Jan and Laurence have been in getting the computer to function so that this book could be finished.

Enormous thanks go to Christ Church, Matchborough, for being willing to finance the printing of the book, and thanks go to my friend Ian for proof reading the text.

# PREFACE

All of us are on a journey. Parts of my journey have been very painful to write about, but if they are of some help to others on their journey then this will have been worth it. I believe that the most important part of our journey lies in our childhood because what happens to us then influences so much of what comes afterwards.

I have tried to recollect things as best I can and each chapter chronicles important years. At the end of each chapter there is a pause for Reflections. This gave me an opportunity to think about some issues that arose and write down some thoughts. I hope that you find them helpful.

My wife Charm has written a chapter on her insights into the journey we have shared and my children have contributed to a chapter on theirs. I really hope that these will be of benefit to many.

I dedicate this book to Charm and our family without whom my journey would have been very different. Words cannot express my love and gratitude. I have called my journey "unusual" because if you read on you will find that I came to a crossroad, and the decision I made there changed my life. I could have made a different decision and I dread to think what would have happened. The path I took was definitely unusual, and although at times I wanted to go back, I'm forever grateful that I walked this path. I also dedicate this book to all who have joined me on my journey and I thank you for walking with me.

Do join me on my journey and may it help you on yours.
Andy Kelso                                      June 2009

# THE AUTHOR

Andy Kelso was Vicar of Christ Church, Matchborough, Redditch, for nearly twenty years. It is a thriving community church in the middle of two estates. He is now Chaplain to Worcester Warriors Rugby Club.

Before becoming a Vicar he was Head of Drama at a London School, and prior to that he was an actor, writer and director, running his own Theatre Company.

He has had two books published, one being a collection of sketches, and more recently a book called "Too many questions, not enough answers, or are there?" which has created a lot of interest.

Andy is married to Charm, who is a Clinical Nurse Specialist in Palliative Care, and they have five children and a growing band of grandchildren!

Andy likes writing, gardening, painting, walking, and playing golf, which keeps him humble! He and Charm are keen Worcester Warriors supporters which means high blood pressure and chewed finger nails! Andy also loves Yorkshire tea, being one of only a few people who have seen the tea plantations on the Yorkshire Moors!

**Chapter One:**

## BEGINNINGS (1947-1965)

My most unusual journey began in Scarborough, North Yorkshire, on November 14th 1947 when I was born. This meant that I was eligible to play cricket for Yorkshire, but sadly, the call never came!

Not long after I was born my parents took my elder brother and I to live in what was then called Southern Rhodesia, now Zimbabwe. My mother was desperate to start a new life away from her roots, thinking that this would save her marriage.

She had been brought up in a wealthy family near Wetherby, North Yorkshire, and the person she was going to marry was killed at Dunkirk. She adored her father who was very English and somewhat eccentric. Like Mr. Bennett in Pride and Prejudice he spent a lot of time in his study to avoid his wife who was quite a hypochondriac. He even took himself off to remote places in the world and was once captured by the Zulus who were very taken with him, so he returned as an honorary Zulu chief with all the regalia! Sadly, he died before I knew him due to having given his gas mask to one of his men in the First World War causing his lungs to be destroyed.

My mother subsequently got married on the rebound, and as it turned out, disastrously, to a tennis professional. He was by all accounts dashing but he had a fearsome temper, drank heavily and was looking to get his hands on my mother's money.

Whilst in Rhodesia things went from bad to worse, until one night, fearing for her life and ours after he tried to strangle her, my mother fled the country with us. She went first to Ireland where she had friends and then returned to Scarborough.

My first memory, when I was about five, was of my mother screaming down the phone in the hallway. I saw a bloody arm waving wildly through the smashed glass pane in the front door. I found out later that this was my father who had found us. I think he would have killed my mother if he had got in, and possibly me as well, but the police arrived first.

Looking back I think my mother had some kind of breakdown. Anyway, it wasn't long before I was packed off to a boarding school at six years old. I'd like to say that I enjoyed it and that school was the happiest time of my life but I'd be lying. I have no real happy memories of this first boarding school. I'm sure there must have been some because I was there for quite a few years, but I really don't remember any.

I do remember being beaten and spending many occasions outside the headmaster's study and, looking back I'm not sure about him as he liked to have the young boys swim in the nude in the pool. There was a teacher who delighted in smacking you over the head with a large book, and my uselessness at maths started here, when I would get beaten for getting my sums wrong. I don't remember much about the school holidays either. They weren't happy times on the whole because my mother wasn't a maternal type. She had a large circle of friends and a busy social calendar, involving a lot of golf, and I'm sure the school holidays cramped her style! When I say I have no happy memories of my life then, two have just returned to me and they highlight some key issues.

At my boarding school I was once quarantined with jaundice and on another occasion with scarlet fever and I remember a young deputy matron who was so kind to me that I wanted to stay in that room forever. In the school holidays I remember regularly visiting my mother's builder with a plate of food provided by her because he didn't look after himself. He was a real craftsman but a recluse. I identified with him and he with me.

So the years passed and I went to public school in my brother's footsteps. He found school to be quite a substitute for home and fitted in really well. I didn't! Being shouted at on the parade ground by some jumped-up idiot didn't go down well, nor did being a fag for some older boy. I remember being hit around the head with a Bunsen–burner tube by a sadistic physics teacher. Life was pretty miserable until one day light shone in my darkness.

My mother had an elder sister who lived in Switzerland and she persuaded my mother that my reformation would only take place if I was educated there. So to Switzerland I went at the age of fourteen, to a skiing resort above Lake Geneva, to an international school that promised to make men out of its pupils. Just before I arrived my mother sent me to a family in France who lived in a chateau. The idea was to learn some French. Fortunately, an American family had the same idea for their daughter and we got on really well – in English!

Suddenly school was fun! I didn't do a lot of work but I did play hard! I took to skiing as a duck to water and before long found myself in the downhill racing team. I took to ice-hockey as well and all manner of sports, and I came alive to girls!

Now, as you know, Switzerland is renowned for its finishing schools and since I'd only just started my proper education I wanted to find out what a finishing school was! My way of doing this was to volunteer for expeditions. These were supposed to be a test of character up in the mountains, camping out and using your resources. My idea of an expedition was to camp near a finishing school and get to know the inmates! My expeditions became very popular and after a while these headed not up into the mountains but down into the bright lights of Geneva!

I remember at the end of one school year, just before I left, that the school erupted with laughter when I was awarded the top prize for expeditions and mountaineering, the Bouquetin Award, which is a mountain goat!

I spent four years at school in Switzerland but now I had to pay the price. I hadn't done enough work! My school reports spelt out the bad news: "Could do so much better! Won't get any exams at this rate! Will never make anything of himself!"

So with a sad heart I left the ski slopes and finishing schools and I was sent to what is affectionately known as a "Crammer" where you cram your head full of facts in a very short time. It was run by some ex-army people and I remember it being a bit like a prison. In order to get out at the weekend you had to have written permission.....mmmm!

Not far away was a girls public school and it didn't take long for me to become very friendly with one of the girls, so friendly in fact that her mother invited me to stay at weekends! They had lots of money and a fantastic place with a swimming pool and for a while everything was rosy, but I messed things up when I started to date another girl from the same school. It turned out to be a disaster. I was nearing the end of my year, with exams looming, when one night a couple of us decided to meet up with the girls nearby. Unfortunately, they got caught climbing back in and they named us! I was hauled up before the commandant and expelled.

You can imagine how this went down with my mother. I remember a difficult meeting with my aunt and uncle in London who lectured me on how I had brought disgrace to the family. Fortunately, the French teacher took pity on me and invited me to stay so that I could do my exams. Unfortunately I didn't repay him very well because after four years in French-speaking Switzerland and one year at a crammer I still failed my A level! I did get some others though.

What happened next is a little bit hazy. I remember being told that it would be good for me to do some voluntary work abroad and so I found myself in a hospital in Germany as an orderly. My German was awful so I don't think that I was of much use to anyone. What made it worse was that I travelled back on the day England beat Germany in the World Cup Final and I missed it!

Around this time I started writing and I managed to persuade some friends to be in a play called "The Last Hour". I was eighteen and we put it on in a loft area above my mother's garage. There were two performances, seventy people came, and it was a great success. The play itself was thoroughly depressing, depicting the last moments on earth of three people following a nuclear holocaust, but I had caught the theatre bug!

I remember helping at Alan Ayckbourn's Theatre in the Round in Scarborough and meeting its founder Stephen Joseph and I realized I wanted to be an actor. Unfortunately, my mother didn't see acting as a proper job and certainly not as a just reward for the thousands spent on my education, so I was told that I needed to go to university.

My brother was now at medical school in London with his career mapped out, whereas my career was far from clear. I remember some strings being pulled to get me to take an entrance exam to Cambridge which I failed! So I had to apply to other universities and in the meantime get a job.

My mother knew the headmaster of a local private school and so I joined the staff as a student teacher. My time there brought about one of the most painful episodes in my life but also one which would have the most far-reaching consequences.

# REFLECTIONS

Any of you reading this will realise that my childhood was unhappy. I think the overriding feeling that I remember was one of loneliness. As I said earlier, my mother wasn't maternal and that caused me great sadness. I know she thought she did the best for me, sending me to boarding schools, but all I wanted was a loving home, and a loving mother. In the 1950's divorce was still quite rare so I was the odd one out at school and I desperately wanted a father like the other boys. Years later my brother Robin had a serious talk with my mother and he was able to tell her some home truths, which wasn't easy. For my part, I would have given up being sent to one of the most expensive schools in the world (even the skiing!) for a loving home life, a local school and friends.

I realized that my father didn't care about me and this caused a lot of problems, both in my childhood and later on, as you will find out. Nowadays there's a lot spoken about the effects of divorce on children, but in my childhood you were expected to get on with life. I was brought up in the era where boys don't cry. I didn't, but I was storing up a lot of problems for the future.

Ever since that first memory of my father trying to break in I became fearful of the dark, and being alone in it. My mother didn't understand but I remember when I was left alone I would stay outside as long as possible, and then when I did come in I would look in every cupboard and under every bed and be so afraid until I heard her return.

One thing I did develop as a child was a good imagination. I had to because I spent a lot of time on my own. That fertile imagination would direct my steps over the next few years.

As you have read, my school years until Switzerland were not fun. I was always being compared to my brother, badly! His reports were glowing, mine were awful.

He seemed to find a niche in school life, a real substitute for a lack of home life, and I didn't. I very quickly became the black sheep of the family. I was told on numerous occasions that I let my mother down, and this didn't help relationships. So all in all I was destined to be a rebel, and what a time to be one in the Swinging Sixties!

My final reflection on this early part of my life is to do with love and values in childhood. The child that each of us once was remains inside us, and becomes part of our identity for the rest of our lives. We can try to bury memories but what has happened to us dictates to a very large extent who we are. This means that parenthood is such an important role, for parents are shaping the lives of their children.

None of us are perfect, far from it, so good enough parenting is good enough! Children mature properly when they know that they belong, that they are special, that they are loved. Qualities of love and caring are formed in a child when they see them functioning in their parents' lives. A child needs to know that they are loved unconditionally, no matter what they do.

I believe with all my heart that God knew exactly what He was doing when He ordained marriage between a man and a woman and told them to be fruitful. There are many single parents who do a fantastic job but it is not God's ideal. A child needs a loving father and mother with the different attributes that they bring. Parenthood is not a hobby. It's an awesome privilege and responsibility and God has entrusted that child to us.

A child's concept of love, of self-worth, of belonging, of sharing, is all formed in childhood. A child's concept of who God is and what is the purpose of life is shaped in childhood. A child's heart is like wax and the impressions made on it will last forever.

Most of us become what those in our childhood told us we would become. We can pretend otherwise and put on our masks and even fool most people, but in our heart when we're alone, our self-image is that given to us in childhood.

Children need roots and wings. This is what good enough parenting is all about. Children need to know that they belong, that they're special. They need to be nurtured in love and acceptance and given good values. Then they need to be given a vision, of who they can become. They need dreams to dream that are not laughed at. They need to be taught life-skills so that they can survive as adults, and they need to be taught to face up to challenges for life is a challenge. But all the time they need to know that they are loved.

Much of what happened to me over the next few years came about because I didn't know that I was loved and I was desperate for love. I believe that each one of us is created in God's image, and God is love, so that means that love is vital to our well-being. We were created to love and be loved but if that love is absent or perverted in our childhood then we will grow up with major problems and other lives will be affected too.

My journey tells you about some of those problems but also offers hope that we don't have to be a prisoner of our past. The greatest gift that my parents gave me was life. Over the next few years I often wished that they hadn't and I came very close to killing myself, but someone had other ideas.

# Chapter Two:

## THE ROLLERCOASTER YEARS
## (1965 – 1973)

I was eighteen years old, my life stretched out in front of me, and it was the swinging sixties! But there was a great emptiness in me. I knew that I had a leaning towards Theatre and the Arts but I needed guidance, and more than anything else I was desperate for a father's care.

I got very friendly with one of the staff during my gap year. He was nearly twenty years older than me, very caring, well-read in the arts, and a growing bond developed. As you can guess he quickly became like a father to me and for a while I was on top of the world. He brought me alive to qualities inside myself that had been dormant. He awoke in me a love of theatre and literature and brought friendship and love to my heart.

But then he told me that he was a homosexual and he wanted to have a physical relationship with me. My world fell apart. I knew that I wasn't a homosexual, although for a time I battled many doubts. I had looked up to this man as a father figure, and I had poured out my heart and soul to him, and now I didn't know what to do. I was an anguished soul. For the first time in my life I had found real love and friendship, and now this relationship was soured, but I didn't want to lose it.

Around this time I bought a motorbike, a big black beast called a Dayton Albatross. One Sunday morning I went for a ride high above Scarborough out in the country. I wanted to think, and I wanted to escape. I remember turning the throttle up and feeling the wind in my hair, as in those days you didn't have to wear a crash helmet! I rounded a corner flanked by trees on both side, suddenly the wind got up and I got into a big wobble! I knew that I was going to come off as I was going too fast and there was nothing I could do. It was as if time slowed right down to a crawl. The next moment the bike veered and I went over the handlebars. I bounced down the road and finally ended up in a ditch.

I came to in utter fear. I thought I was going to die. Blood was pouring from my head and the friction had ripped a lot of my clothes from me. I remember looking up and seeing a cow chewing the cud and I thought, "I don't want to die!" I staggered up and at that point I cried out, "God, I don't want to die! Help me!" I was in the middle of nowhere. There were no cars, just a farmhouse across a field. Somehow I managed to stagger to it, knocked on the door, and collapsed. It was a good job they were Yorkshire folk! Heaven knows what a sight I looked and how I must have alarmed them! I was taken down to the hospital and I don't remember much else. What I do remember though is my mother coming to see me and berating me for being so stupid. I think she was shocked and this was her response, but I didn't need it. By contrast, my friend arrived and showed great care and concern. I went home eventually but developed serious delayed shock. It had been a traumatic accident and suddenly it just enveloped me. People seemed distant and yet their voices were too loud. I would get the shakes and I didn't know what was going on.

Unfortunately, my mother's doctor was of the old school. If you didn't have anything physically wrong with you then you were fine. I was given a lecture about how I had let my mother down again, how I needed to be more like my brother, and instructed to pull myself together. Looking back now I'm staggered at this response! I had had a serious accident that should have killed me. I appeared to recover well and then slumped. I don't think you need to be a brain surgeon to work it out! The result of all this was that I was forced to return to my job in no fit state, and the only person who showed me any care and compassion was my teacher friend. I think I could have convinced myself that I was a homosexual after all but I was in no state for more trauma.

I had applied to various universities and finally got a place at London, to do an English degree. I was still in a real mess and no one knew this except my friend. Part of his concern meant that he gave up his job and got a new one in London to follow me. I didn't know what to do. This was one of the lowest points in my life.

I went down to London and for a while stayed in my aunt's flat as she was abroad. I threw myself into writing a play called "The Wasted Wheel". I suppose it was a real attempt to release some of my pain. It's a historical drama based around the characters of Richard the Second and Henry Bolingbroke who usurps the throne. Later on it would be produced on the London fringe but I didn't know that then.

Let me quote to you one or two speeches and you'll see how they mirrored my soul. The young queen, Isabella, pouring out her heart says:

"But something passes down from age to age, something that will never lose its lustre, the love that is in a human heart, felt for a human being, the feelings in a human soul that can never reach the tongue. But they are far, far deeper than can ever be expressed in words. Though in the end we may return to where we started out, it is with deeper knowledge and a clearer vision, and what we find is that a human being, though stripped of all he has upon that path he trod, still has a heart, still has a soul, still has those feelings that can never be expressed."

The tortured King Richard reflects:

"Is it only through suffering that men will understand? Is it only when one can say 'I have suffered and thus I know' is life as hard as that? I think it is. And yet to end it all, the last ironic twist, that even when we've suffered, we alone are

11

wiser, sadder, sometimes broken, and others only learn by treading that track that we have trod. Are you wiser Richard now? "Yes! Wiser, sadder, and broken".

The play has always been special for me, a friend at a dark time. I was nineteen years old.

At the beginning of my degree course I lived in a hall of residence and cut myself off from others. I saw my friend occasionally but I was in more and more turmoil. It's impossible to describe how I felt at that time. I can only say that it was like hell on earth. My heart and my soul had gone into this friendship. He was like a father to me, the father I had always wanted. Apart from this friendship I was alone, but I knew that deep down I could no longer see him because I was not a homosexual and that was the relationship that he wanted. I loved him deeply but not in that way and the pain of never seeing him again was crushing. I threw myself into sports and for a while played rugby at Wasps. I tackled ferociously and tried to excel at fly half, and I guess I was letting all my anger and frustration loose! I moved into digs for a time and felt even more lonely. At times I was quite suicidal. Rugby was a great outlet for me until I ended up in hospital with bruised kidneys and torn lumbar muscles.

When I went back into the hall of residence I was befriended by two fellow students called John and Charm. I wasn't an easy person to befriend! It turned out that they were Christians. Now I vaguely thought that most people were Christians but the difference with them was that they really believed it all! I kept my guard up and gave them a hard time. They talked to me about God as a father and God as love and I didn't want to know. My image of God as a loving father was so hurt and damaged. All their talk was really a waste of time but I did value their concern which I saw was genuine.

What struck me was that they lived out their faith. Over a while we became friends and then friendship with Charm developed into a relationship. I'd first noticed her in the TV lounge when some of us were watching a rugby international and she was the only girl present. Being Cornish she loved rugby and our first date later on was to go to a rugby match!

In the early days of our relationship I wasn't the best company. There was still a lot of pain and hurt and anger in me, but Charm stuck by me because she was in love. I peppered her with lots of questions about God and the Bible and this went on for some time.

In the Easter holidays of my final year I went back to Yorkshire and Charm went to Cornwall. On my return I collected her from the station and I told her that I wouldn't have come back if it hadn't been for her. She blurted out that she couldn't help me anymore and only Jesus could. Amazingly, I replied that I knew that! The remainder of the journey from Paddington to Kilburn passed in silence. I think I needed that ultimatum as I had been mulling over things for ages. I remember returning to my room and getting on my knees and crying out to God. I said something like "God, if you're there, if you're who Charm says you are, and if you can turn my life around then please come into my heart. I'm sorry where I've messed things up but please help me."

There were no flashing lights, no angels at the window, but in that moment I knew that something had happened. So did Charm because I told her that I was going to be Archbishop of Canterbury! What had happened? Well, God started to become real and the Bible was no longer a dusty old closed book. This was an enormous upheaval!

It was just before my finals and I was planning a career in the theatre. I had got a place at the Bristol Old Vic Theatre School and now God had come into my life!

Suddenly I wanted people to know about Jesus, how he could change your outlook on life, what He had done for them on the Cross and what He could do for them now. I struggled through my Finals (no continuous assessment then!) and had to return to Yorkshire to a summer job.

My world was turned upside down! I wrote to Charm and told her that I was going to go into the Church. This was crisp because I'd hardly ever been to church and knew nothing about it! She told me to be careful because not every vicar I would meet was a Christian. I thought this was strange and didn't know what she meant but I would find out!

So I gave up my place at drama school, much to my mother's amazement! She had no idea what was going on and I think she thought I had now become seriously deranged! The local vicar wanted to be shot of my enthusiasm and so he sent me to see the Bishop's right hand man. I remember thinking that he looked like Dracula in his long black robes and on and on he went. After a while I interrupted him and asked if he was a Christian! This didn't go down well and I was told that I needed experience before thinking of applying for the Church!

So over the next year I got lots of experience! I got a job on the North Sea Gas pipelines. They thought that a person with a degree should be in the office. I assured them that Maths was not my strong point and I would prefer to do manual work. They disagreed and I was placed in the office dealing with wages. I made such a mess of it that an accountant had to come from London to sort it out so I went onto the line! I would take every opportunity to share my new-found faith and I should have taken more seriously the greeting that met me on most mornings "Hey-up! It's the vicar!"

With that experience behind me I set off back to London where I got a job in what was then known as The Spastics Society (now Scope). I was employed as driver and general help and I had a little room in the basement. I soon got to know my way around the London sights and gave tours, making up what I didn't know! One day I found an old teddy bear in the dustbin outside and it was like a visual aid to me. I named him Fitzroy because that was the name of the Square in which I worked. He was washed and years later given new eyes, nose and stuffing from someone who knew all about bears. I eventually placed a tag around his neck which read: "Hello. In 1971 I was rescued from a dustbin in London. I was given a new life because I was loved. Miracles like this can happen to you too because Jesus loves you." Fitzroy is about ninety years old and is the custodian of our downstairs loo!

I was living in a flat near Kings Cross and going to church at All Souls near Oxford Street, trying to learn more about Jesus. It was now 1971 and I was in my Sonny of Sonny and Cher mode – long hair, kaftan style clothes, platforms, quite a hippie really! The vicar, John Stott, obviously saw something beneath all this and really helped me.

I wanted to use my dramatic gifts to put across the Christian message and I teamed up with my flat mate, who played the guitar, and we started to do gigs at coffee bars and other venues and it was exciting. I was seeing Charm at weekends and rugby was still a passion as I was playing for an old boys' side now with my good friend Peter Jones and there was a lot of camaraderie between wives and girlfriends. Returning from rugby on a Saturday we would often go to a little bistro near South Kensington called the Vino Bistro. It had great food, was cheap, and you could bring your own wine. Unfortunately, on one occasion, someone broke into the car and stole my rugby kit and Charm's prized maxi-coat which had been hand made by her grandmother!

I had a couple of great old cars in those days. The first was a Morris Minor, built like a tank, and called Samantha. It was stolen from me and used in a robbery. I got it back and then painted the family crest on both doors so that it stood out. The second car was an old Volkswagen that you could hear coming and that too had the crest on both doors.

I felt an increased calling to harness my dramatic gifts with the Gospel, but I realized that I needed a much better knowledge of the Bible and so I went to a theological college in Nottingham for a year. I was put on some tedious Diploma course at the university and realized this was not for me so I told the Principal that I was leaving. His name was Michael Green, a tremendous person, and he saw what I needed so he made up a course for me! I used to go with him on his missions and I would have one-to-one sessions with him about how to bring the Gospel to difficult people! I got the opportunity to write for radio and I really benefited from the year.

I was teamed up halfway through the year with a guy from Canada who had been invited to come over to the college, having recommitted himself as a Christian after having been challenged by Michael when he was on a tour in Canada. He was a bear of a man who had become disillusioned, left the ministry and his family, hit the bottle and become a down and out. He was very intense but so likeable and we teamed up really well, although he didn't suffer fools gladly, thinking that most of the students were a waste of time. He wanted to tell everyone about Jesus and he did, whether they wanted to hear or not!

Through all my ups and downs Charm had put up with me and whilst at college, before my course had been revamped, I proposed to her. She said (and still says!) that it was because I was miserable! I was still a mixed-up person and Charm would have to suffer that for a long while yet.

Charm had completed her degree and the year I was in Nottingham she was in Birmingham working at the University with Campus Crusade for Christ. At the end of the year we were both jobless and penniless but had a wedding planned for September! We had to get some money, so Charm worked in a laundry in Birmingham and I became a night security guard in Aston, Birmingham. It was terrible! It was just a sop to the insurance company really. You had to patrol this vast site and clock into dark buildings and offices. I was a nervous wreck and was so glad when I could leave.

We were to be married in Mawnan in Cornwall at a little church overlooking the Helford River. The date was fixed for September $2^{nd}$ 1972. There was just one problem – my mother refused to come! As far as she was concerned I would be marrying beneath me and this was not acceptable. I did think this was hypocritical from someone who had married a tennis player! She finally relented and grudgingly came. Looking back I can understand some of her concern. We were young, I had no job, and we had nowhere to live yet!

We were offered a friend's house in Suffolk for our honeymoon, but as it turned out Charm was offered a teaching post in London and so our honeymoon was one night in a pub near Dartmoor! For two weeks we commuted from Suffolk to London every day, Charm going to a nightmare of a school in Wembley and me tramping the streets trying to find somewhere to live. We then moved in with some student friends in Northwood, but just three weeks after our wedding Charm's beloved Dad died suddenly from a heart attack and we journeyed back to Cornwall. This was so sad so soon after our wedding and I was so sorry not to have been able to get to know him. When we returned we managed to rent a house in

Harrow Wealdstone. I had gained a place at a Drama School in London as I wanted to combine my acting skills with my Christian beliefs.

Soon after our marriage Charm became pregnant with our first child, Brandon, who was born in August 1973. We had to leave our house so now we were homeless with a baby and two puppies! Little did we know that things would get worse before they got better – more rollercoaster years!

## REFLECTIONS

I've said quite a few times that I was desperate for love. Because my mother wasn't maternal I didn't feel loved by her and there was an aching void where my father's love should have been. My teacher friend filled the void but there were strings attached if this relationship was to continue and I couldn't go down that road. Much later on I understood a vital truth. The core factor for people getting into the bondage of homosexuality is seeking an unfulfilled relationship with their father.

That's why parenting is so vital. Today we have so many absent fathers, or fathers who don't spend time with their children and we're storing up trouble. Kids get into gangs as a substitute for what's lacking in the home, often with devastating consequences. They've had no role model and so it's easy for them to think that they can do what they want, but there's always a cost. After twenty five years of working on council estates I've seen the fallout time and again. Kids get hooked on drugs, drink, crime, and sex is just gratification. When a baby arrives the girl is left on her own and the whole cycle repeats itself.

There's a generation of children who have no real concept of love, so they're prey to whoever is out there with another agenda. We've had a government that has fallen over backwards to help single mothers and they've penalized marriage. The result is that we have a society in moral collapse.

A stable family makes for a stable society. Every civilization has collapsed when the foundation of family life is destroyed. My story can be repeated thousands of times and with far worse outcomes and it doesn't need to be so, not if parents took their responsibility seriously.

I believe that every baby born is a gift from God and parents are the stewards of that baby. What every child needs to know in the depths of their soul is that they are loved uniquely. I didn't know that I was loved and so I looked for love elsewhere. My search led me to so much pain and confusion that I nearly killed myself. I had love offered to me but it turned out to be twisted and that led me to put up barriers around my heart.

You see there are so many consequences to all of this and my childhood and early adulthood are living proof. Each child is unique and therefore deals with situations differently. My brother and I are good examples of this. What deeply affected me didn't affect him in the same way. We paid the price differently, but there was still a price for us both.

I'm so grateful to God for bringing Charm into my life for she loved me through it all, but then there was a cost for her of loving me because my journey into some kind of maturity caused her much pain.

When I knelt on the floor and asked Jesus into my life there was a change, but it took a long time for major areas of my life to be healed. There was no magic wand. It's a bit like being a baby all over again. Your spirit has come alive to God but it's all new and you need help. Old patterns didn't just disappear. They got buried a bit and then resurfaced.

God's not in the business of superficial things. Generally speaking, the deeper the hurt and trauma the longer it's going to take to heal. The fact is that God wants us to be healed so that we can reach out to others who are hurting. Sometimes we don't get the full measure of healing that we'd like but we have to trust that God knows what He is doing.

When I married Charm in 1972 I thought I had got my life in some sort of order. But deep down I hadn't and I was still a danger. Sadly, Charm paid the price as you'll find out. Being married for so long now and having five wonderful children and now grandchildren, I've gained a lot of healing from my past, but over the years major problems that have happened to me find their roots in my childhood and early years.

If you're reading this as a parent please take note, and don't think it's too late!

**Chapter Three:**

## MORE ROLLERCOASTER YEARS (1973 – 1983)

Amazingly, a friend from drama school and her husband took us in for a while. Looking back it was so kind of them but we couldn't stay there forever. We were offered accommodation in an old Victorian house in Lewisham, South London, in exchange for looking after the ninety three year old occupant! We had no choice so off we went!

Before we travel there I have to touch on my drama student days. I was really grateful to be able to go to drama school since I thought I had lost that opportunity. I really enjoyed the course but I caused Charm great pain by engaging in a couple of wrong relationships. I make no excuses, I was to blame, but Charm stood by me and we moved on. I was still desperately immature and mixed-up.

When I left drama school I was employed by the Christian Arts Project as their Drama Director. This was a new venture of exploring drama and the arts in worship and evangelism and I was to form my own theatre group and try to take the nation by storm! My salary was minimal (under the tax threshold!) and we were naïve. My contract stated that they would fund accommodation costs. We found a place to live that only cost £8 a week but the trustees refused to pay, which is why we ended up in Lewisham.

It was not a good time, especially for Charm. It was winter and the house was freezing. There was even ice inside the windows! Worse, the house was overrun by mice. We would come down in the mornings to find mice on the kitchen table. It was so cold that we all slept in the same bed – Charm and I, the baby and two dogs!

I was busy with my job and Charm was very lonely. One evening I returned to find she'd been locked in the living room because our ninety year old locked all the doors before he went to bed!

I was excited about the job. I had formed a theatre group and we'd started to get bookings. At that time there were no other Christian groups like us functioning. Most churches were welcoming, although a few vicars thought drama and dance were of the devil! The Project was launched in Birmingham with Cliff Richard and others and we quickly found out that we had to be adaptable!

We would perform in cathedrals and tiny churches. Charm got involved which was good for her but it meant someone had to take Brandon, our baby, from her when she went on stage! We started travelling a lot, performing and taking drama workshops. Our fame spread because we were invited to perform at the Royal Albert Hall. We just took it in our stride and enjoyed every moment. It was after that event that we came out to find the dogs had been sick in the car and we had to push the car to get it started!

We had a sound engineer who liked to create amazing special effects and I remember being asked to write a piece on Paul's shipwreck. Those who were there that night never forgot it! We were at the Central Westminster Hall in London and it wasn't long before the stage was awash with water as the cast had to constantly put their heads into buckets of water at the back of the stage. The ship's captain got stage fright and was rooted to the spot and the sound effects were out of this world, to such an extent that we never got invited back!

The theatre group was great, a real family. I managed to pull together the most unlikely people and they all came good. We had a superb stage manager and I had a great time writing different material. No venue was seen as too difficult, we just saw it as a challenge. We even got invited to Belfast at the height of the troubles!

However, the Christian Arts Project were running out of money, we couldn't live on thin air and nor could we continue to live in Bleak House! In those days young Mums didn't expect to go back to work after having a baby. Charm didn't want to but she was desperate and started applying for teaching jobs. She was offered an interview in Harrow at a secondary modern which was about to become comprehensive. When phoning to confirm her attendance for interview she mentioned that I was also looking for a job and was told to 'bring me along'! When we arrived for the interview the Head of Department was a Christian and it was all very informal! It was February, the original advert was for the Autumn Term but we were both offered posts for the Summer Term, a matter of weeks away! It was to be a long commute again! Not knowing what to do Charm rang Trevor the vicar in Harrow Wealdstone to inquire about the possibility of someone in the church child-minding Brandon while we were at work. Within hours Eldey, his wife, had phoned back not only offering to look after Brandon herself but also storage space (we still didn't have much!) and accommodation! This is how we ended up in a caravan in their garden with all our worldly goods in part of their shed! We are still so grateful for the kindness they showed us, especially as we didn't know them well at all, having been very irregular church attenders when living in Harrow Wealdstone.

It was while we were trying to find their house when living there that I nearly ran over a policeman! This person stepped out into the road and I had to avoid him. The next minute a police car came up behind us. The officer asked if I had seen him trying to flag me down to tell me that my lights weren't working! He asked me what the registration number was and I got out, had a look and told him! He was getting exasperated and asked to see some identification. I pointed to the family crest on the door and at that point he'd had enough! What we didn't know was that we were right outside the vicarage and they'd seen the whole thing!

So started a new phase of life! That's how I fell into teaching on a temporary basis that lasted ten years! Amazing isn't it! And that's how we managed to buy our own house in North Watford for ten thousand pounds!

I had a few temporary appointments, and nearly got a job at Eton, until I finally got a job at Harrow County Boys School. They were keen to develop drama and so I became the Drama Department! It was a battle for survival because I used to get all the kids that couldn't do anything else! Eventually I turned some mobile classrooms into a drama block one summer holiday and for a while never looked back. I developed a whole curriculum and, because I was situated away from the main school, different rules applied! If kids messed around I would physically throw them out and warn them never to return. They didn't! Having said that, I set the standard high and most kids responded well. Eventually the work they achieved was amazing and drama became very popular.

I continued to run the theatre group at evenings and weekends and then we tried our hand at Street Theatre. Actually it was forced on us because the church where we were rehearsing didn't look favourably on drama, the vicar that is! So we went outside! Now Watford had a precinct closed to traffic so it was ideal, and most Saturday mornings we'd be there performing.

At that time Watford were in the same league as Chelsea and Chelsea were then renowned for their fans, skinheads and boot-boys! We got a write-up in the local paper for bringing calm to the fans before the game! What happened was that we did a sketch on the Good Samaritan and the Samaritan was a punk-rocker, which went down really well with the fans!

Street Theatre is a great discipline because you have to be sharp and deal with the unexpected. It was an excellent preparation for the pantomimes which followed. I remember that we were invited to the Richmond Horse Show to do a bit of drama! Various local groups had tents there and the Church's tent was as far away from the people as possible. We looked around to see where the ice-cream sellers were and decided to use a double-glazing van as our backdrop. We'd recently acquired a big red door on a frame and we were arguing about where to put it when we noticed a crowd had gathered! Cue for action!

We had lots of great times and some disastrous moments. One of the most memorable was on April Fool's Day when we were performing outside. One of the cast has been accused of some crime or other and was to be drenched in water and then have eggs thrown at him and flour. One of the cast from the audience came forward and said that he would take his place. Everything was going well until, completely covered in eggs and flour, he lowered his head and the last barrage hit an immaculately dressed couple! She was wearing a mink coat and it turned out that he was an ex-boxing champion! The local church got the bill for cleaning and the couple never forgot the drama!

We lived in Watford for nine years and our second son, Barney, and our eldest daughter, Tammy, were born there. They were mainly happy times but it was also where I had a major bout of depression. I'd had depression when I was working in London but this time it was worse.

Depression is a terrible thing. I don't mean feeling a little down, I mean real depression, and sadly I have been prone to it over the years. Some of it was triggered by an energetic workload that suddenly became too much, but some of it was about my past rearing its head.

Suddenly you're locked into yourself and it's a downward spiral into a never-ending black hole. It's a living hell. I had to force myself to do things for others and every time it was a monumental effort. In those days there wasn't the understanding or the treatment that there is today, and some idiot would tell you to snap out of it. If you could you would, I assure you, but at the time it's impossible. What made it worse was that Charm had just started training as a nurse and we had three young children. I did get through it eventually and returned to my job.

Life in the community was fun. We'd had a wonderful playgroup for the children and I decided to write a little pantomime that we parents could put on for the children. It became so successful that we put on a panto annually and the community came. They continued it long after we left. There's a lot of talent in people and it's about drawing it out as I was to find out years later.

Charm and I were going to a church just outside Watford and the vicar dropped a bombshell! He suggested that I really ought to think about full-time ministry in the Church, which meant becoming a vicar! My teaching career was fast coming to an end. I was running out of energy. I had put so much into it and the end was dramatic. We wanted to raise some money for film equipment, and I hit on the idea of a Dramathon! We hoped to get into the Guinness Book of Records by staging seventy five hours of non-stop drama. It took a lot of organizing and persuasion and we got some celebrities along to open it. The kids did really well. They were all split into groups and time slots and the staff also put on a concert over three nights where I foolishly agreed to be involved in every other act!

I was so exhausted in the planning of it that I ended up in hospital, but like all good troupers I staggered in to do my bit every night. We raised lots of money for local charities and we bought our film equipment, but I'd had it, and that was the end of my teaching career!

I went to a three day selection conference with regard to being trained as a vicar. I remember that on the final day the chairman said to me "Let's face it, you're the kind of person who sticks two fingers up to the establishment! Am I right?" I replied that I hoped I wouldn't do that, but his assessment was right. The chairman said "Good! We need people like you in the Church of England!" I'd been accepted!

Our life was going to be turned upside down once again. We had three young children, Charm was still doing her nurse training, and our life in Watford was about to end. The problem was that we didn't get any real advice so before we knew it we were selling our house, buying one in Nottingham, transferring Charm's training, and trying to find new schools. In hindsight we should have stayed put, and I could have gone to a London college, or at the very least we should have rented out our house. But we didn't!

We moved to Nottingham and I found myself back at the same Bible college that I'd been at years before! The problem was that in two years time we'd be moving all over again, uprooting our children and finding that we'd lost most of our money, which is why the title to the next chapter is really fitting!

## REFLECTIONS

I'm sure that some of you can see a pattern emerging already! Sadly, bouts of depression have followed me all my life. The depression I faced in Watford was severe, which is why I can only describe it as hell on earth. I have heard many cruel remarks about depression but I assure you it is a serious illness. I battled every day with that darkness, forcing myself to do things, forcing myself to try and help others, but it took monumental efforts. There were still a lot of unresolved issues going back to my childhood and the depression was a symptom.

Years before when I was at Nottingham I had counselling for my past but all it seemed to do was stir it all up and not resolve anything. Serious depression is one of the worst illnesses. Most people don't understand. People sympathise when you've got something physically wrong with you, but mental illness is another matter. So the sense of isolation is extreme. In my case a lasting effect for ages was panic attacks. Going anywhere where I had to sit down with others was a nightmare.

I cried out to God so much in those days and all too often my prayers seemed to bounce off the ceiling. I wrote a journal of my days and I got some insight into what hell is like. If Heaven is to be with God, and therefore it's a place of love and laughter and goodness and everything that we cherish, then Hell is the opposite. Hell is to be totally self-absorbed, to such an extent that there's no glimmer of light, no hope, no purpose, just anguish, regret, and a never-ending darkness.

I have experienced something of this and I don't want anyone to go to Hell. I didn't get the answers that I wanted from God during all this time, but looking back I was given an insight and experience into what awaits those who reject God's offer of love and salvation through Christ.

Ultimately, we get what we want. If we want to live our lives without reference to God then we'll get an eternity of complete self-centeredness, which is Hell.

To live with someone who is seriously depressed is a difficult thing and I'll leave Charm to express her thoughts about this in a later chapter. Suffice it to say that I'm so grateful to her for her love and support.

Charm taught me about family life and I tried to be a good husband and father. We didn't have much money but we were a family. You have to have energy to look after children and obviously we had lots then! We only had a small back garden so we spent lots of time in the park. On Sundays we'd go swimming, then go to church, have lunch and then go to the park.

Our eldest, Brandon, was into cricket by the age of two! We'd play inside first of all with a plastic skittle and ball, but it wasn't long before we were in the park with a bat and real cricket ball, much to the shock of passers-by! I took them to a nearby playing field in the winter to play football and rugby and they all had to learn how to rugby tackle, including Charm!

We had a lot of fun and I'm sure they have many happy memories of our time there. Christmas was always special because Charm is nuts about it and transforms the house into Santa's grotto! The result is that they still all want to be with us at Christmas. We had wonderful holidays in Cornwall, mainly camping, which is why it is still a favourite destination for us all.

Charm and I had our ups and downs in those early years. I was good at throwing things and she was good at catching or ducking! I had my silent times and we both had times where we wouldn't apologise and I'd try to sleep on the sofa! Hindsight is a wonderful thing but we can lose so much time by not forgiving and forgetting. Life's too short to hold onto resentments. At times marriage isn't easy but unless it's impossible it's worth everything to work at it.

My time with the Christian Arts Project was so much fun, apart from the lack of money. Drama had emerged from the Church and here we were trying to bring it back! I want to so thank those who worked with me at this time because they were a great bunch, willing to do anything. I also remember in our Bleak House days putting together the first Christian Arts magazine. It was called "Gallery" and for a long time I used to write most of the articles under pen names!

There's something about drama that can really engage people and communicate a message. I'm so grateful for those creative years when I could write all kinds of material to try to express the Christian message. Some of those scripts were published in a book called "Scene One" and it was a tribute to members of Domini, our theatre group.

My teaching days were definitely interesting! Drama as a subject was completely new then and untried. Many teachers thought it was a waste of time, which is why I got the pupils who were not very academic, but you'll remember from your schooldays the subjects that you really enjoyed, and one of the main reasons for this was having a teacher who inspired you.

I wanted to inspire my pupils with what drama could do to draw out their gifts and abilities, and years later it was such a thrill to be contacted by a former pupil who remembered his drama teacher inspiring him!

To see pupils who others had given up on produce pieces of work that required discipline, creativity, and teamwork was a real joy and, I might say, a real shock to other teachers! Good teaching is about inspiring pupils, and I was fortunate to have a subject that could draw out creative gifts and which also encouraged a person's character development. It was exhausting but very rewarding.

I had been involved in trying to help the Church rediscover the use of drama. Now I was to train to be a vicar in the Church, and a whole new drama would unfold!

## Chapter Four:

# HELP! WHAT AM I DOING?
## (1983 – 1990)

God's got a great sense of humour! Having waved goodbye to Nottingham over ten years earlier here I was back again. I didn't have a good image of vicars. They always seemed very religious and out of touch. I didn't get the impression that there was a lot of fun in church and I began to have great doubts about this calling.

I don't remember much about the course I did, but I was grateful to those who were with me on it, many of whom had families so that we helped one another out. I know that many students got bogged down in areas which raised more questions than answers and I didn't want to lose my heart for Jesus and the Gospel through analysis leading to paralysis of faith!

I had a good time at the church I was seconded to for training. It was on a local council estate and again it showed God's sense of humour! My upbringing and background were as far removed from a council estate as you can get but for the next twenty five years that would be where I ministered.

I don't really know what my mother thought about all of this. I suppose she was grateful that I was training for "a respectable career". My uncle was highly displeased. I remember when I announced that I was going into the Church that he took me to his club in London and told me that it was a waste of time because I'd never make a Bishop!

Our time at Nottingham went quickly and before we knew it we were looking for a curacy, which is a trainee vicar's post. Nothing materialized for ages until at the last moment I was offered a post in Norfolk – on a council estate!

We'd only been in Nottingham for two years and now it was time to move again. We thought we'd rent out the house to incoming students and then we had to find new schools all over again. Charm had completed her nurse training at the end of my first year and had continued working nights as a Staff Nurse. She was expecting our fourth child when we left Nottingham.

In a later chapter our children will tell you of their memories, and moving schools was not a good one. For reasons that will be made clear they would have to move again in a very short time, and it was extremely painful.

Before you get ordained you have to go on a retreat. A few of us decided to find the nearest pub one evening and it was a long walk, Norfolk miles being what they are! When we finally got back everything was locked and we had to shin up the drainpipe! The next morning I was ordained in Norwich cathedral. I remember a very pompous little man carrying what looked like a mace ordering us about and telling us to follow him in a dignified manner down the aisle. I beckoned to the others to stop and so Mr. Pompous walked off on his own until we eventually followed!

Alarm bells should have rung when the vicar went on holiday just after I arrived and handed me the hospital bleep! Not only was I in charge of the church but I was suddenly the hospital chaplain! This was pretty daunting. I managed to alienate the organist by introducing some choruses for the children on my guitar and I infuriated the vicar on his return by having dared to offer prayer for anyone who wanted it after the services. I couldn't see what all the fuss was about but things didn't improve.

The hospital chaplaincy was new ground for me but very rewarding, apart from being woken up in the middle of the night. There were difficult times when people would blame me for what was happening but all-in-all it was a good learning curve.

In the parish I was asked to look after baptism preparation. I found it difficult because I knew that most people had no idea of what they were promising as parents and godparents, and no intention of keeping those promises. They just wanted the baby 'done'! I wanted to honour God in this, so having dutifully gone through everything with one couple I could see they wanted to leave. I said "OK. I don't think this is getting anywhere so I'm going to pray for you that God will make Himself real. Is that alright?" They nodded, I prayed, and they left.

The next morning the wife rang me up. She said, "You're not going to believe this but Jesus appeared to me last night and I'm a different person, and so is my husband!" I was dumbfounded! God had actually answered my prayer! They became members of the church with an amazing story to tell. He worked on the oil rigs and had a captive audience!

I started up a group in our home for some of the husbands who never came to church. Their wives had been praying for them for years with no results. We got on well and I tried to answer some of their questions.

I remember going to a John Wimber conference in Sheffield and hearing some dynamic teaching about healing and miracles. I thought some of the experiences there were wacky but I realized that Jesus was still in the business of miracles and that most people needed to see them to take Him seriously. I told God that I was open to whatever He wanted to do and I should have realized that this was dangerous!

Not long after returning I was rung up by a local vicar who asked me to come to speak and minister at a healing mission they were holding. I told him that I thought he'd got the wrong person, but he insisted that I come. I was terrified! I invited the group of men and their wives and one of them only came to pour scorn on the whole thing!

I taught about Jesus' miracles and then we had a break for coffee. I nearly forgot! As we were singing at the beginning the scornful husband, who was a real sceptic, suddenly cried out and then collapsed, disappearing out of sight behind the pew! He then started sobbing. His wife was totally amazed! During the coffee time I asked him what had happened and he said that God had touched him. I could hardly believe it, he had only come to gloat!

After the break I knew the moment had come and I couldn't put it off any longer. I had to ask people if they wanted prayer for healing. I prayed that no one would respond or that it would be something small! I opened my eyes to see a couple approaching. He looked really angry and she looked really ill. It turned out that this was their last resort. She had terminal cancer!

I asked one or two of my friends to come and pray with me and we prayed, desperately! Suddenly the husband asked if I could feel the heat. I replied that I couldn't feel anything. The wife said that she felt this amazing heat on her and around her. I was standing about two feet away and didn't feel a thing!

And that's how the evening went on! When we were about to leave I noticed a man sitting all on his own. I asked if he was all right and he nodded. Then he told me that he'd wandered into the church to see what was going on. He wasn't a Christian when he entered. Nobody spoke to him because there was a lot going on, but he'd so sensed God's presence that he'd opened his heart to Jesus. I was truly amazed!

You must realise by now that life in the church was never going to be the same again and unfortunately, the vicar didn't like this. I suppose he felt threatened but what happened next was awful.

I was away at a conference and when I returned Charm told me that there were real problems. It had been discovered that the vicar had been taking advantage of vulnerable women in the church. We invited him around with some others who were aware of the situation and we tried to be supportive, assuring him of God's forgiveness after his admission of guilt and repentance, and of our discretion. Wrong choice! He knew he'd been caught with his trousers down and acted like a little boy who'd been found out stealing. We had believed his pleas for forgiveness but the next moment all hell broke loose!

I was summoned to the Bishop on charges of being insubordinate, and of causing major problems in the church. Stories were circulated that I had practiced black magic on the beach and that either Charm or I or both of us were having affairs! It was unbelievable! The vicar was running scared and sought to turn the tables on me, making up all sorts of allegations. It was a terrible time for us and did great damage. For some unknown reason I chose not to retaliate, not to speak out what had really happened. I can't remember why.

In those days, the vicar was right whatever had happened. I was the lowly curate and so I would have to go. There was great distress in the church and some seriously heated meetings. So many people stood up for me and near the end one of the women from the estate stood up in a service and told the vicar what she thought of him!

It was a terrible ending for what had been some amazing times. Our fourth child, Kimberley, had been born there, three days before Christmas, just after a service where I was dressed up as a clown! Charm was timing the contractions throughout the service and still managed to produce a roast before a quick dash to the hospital! We had seen hardened men come to Christ and God move in amazing ways and perhaps this was the backlash, but yet again we had to move on, and this time it was with such pain.

I was close to giving it all up but others advised me to hang in there however hard it seemed. So we found ourselves in Norwich and guess what? I was asked to take charge of a rundown church on a council estate!

We were moving our children for the third time in four years and it was tough for them. The house we were given was smaller than the one we'd left so this caused problems too. It was a painful time of readjustment and trying to be positive. Brandon found his school change difficult and we had our problems with him. I had the police on the doorstep and parents' evenings were difficult. Being stuck in Norfolk didn't help Brandon's sporting development either.

My brief was to try and bring life to a rundown church on an estate. I worked hard at it and I wish I could remember the different stages but I know there was a lot of prayer! In time it grew into a lively community church. A lot of people became Christians and we had lots of young families.

Some of the men became involved through a football team I started. We decided to enter a team in the Saturday league and because the area where we lived was called Hellesdon we called ourselves the Hellesdon Angels! One of the church members owned the local sports shop and kindly sponsored us with a new kit. It was red and white and we were the smartest team in the league! The problem was that we weren't fit. We could compete until half-time and then we ran out of steam! The result of this was that we didn't win one game in our first year! One morning as I collected the milk from the doorstep there was a bottle of champagne with a note which said that we could only open it when we won a game!

I challenged the players to join me in the park over the summer to get fit and they responded. The result was that we won our first game of the new season and never looked back. Success breeds success and before long we had some really good players. Wives and girlfriends would support us shouting out "Come on you Angels!" It was a lot of fun and the greatest thrill for me was to have Brandon playing alongside me and we even had our Barney playing once or twice. He was still quite young!

Occasionally I would have to rush from the game to take a wedding and this brought puzzled looks from the bride and groom who could smell the muscle liniment I'd rubbed on my legs! That reminds me! The very first wedding I did the bride fainted. I could see it coming and rushed behind her to hold her up!

The football team did a lot of good in drawing people together and it had a big impact on the church.

Our youngest, Bethany, was born in Norwich and so we were now a large family. We started to put down roots which is difficult when you know that you're going to be moving on again, but with a young family it's what happens.

I wanted church to be real, fun, encouraging, challenging, and really the best place to be on a Sunday! I upset some people in the diocese along the way because I've never had much time for the establishment when it's out of touch. I felt that one of the main purposes of the church was to reach out to those who weren't yet in it, and that meant bringing the reality of God into people's lives.

When you're a curate you have to attend all sorts of meetings and, most importantly, post-ordination training, or potty training! I remember being asked to give my tips to new curates on filing post etc. I was the wrong person to ask! I said that I had a great method and they all looked very interested and started to write down notes. I told them that I had three piles on my desk – really important, vaguely important, and not important! When the piles got bigger I threw out the unimportant, by which time the vaguely important was no longer important and the really important was now vaguely important! I told them that it worked really well, but the tutors were not impressed! They were nearly apoplectic when I said that I didn't use a diary! I had really tried but spent too long writing everything in it! I have never missed anything important in twenty five years so my internal diary has worked well!

I had my first real experience of the occult on the estate. I was asked into a house where all sorts of weird things were happening and the family was frightened. I found out that the parents had been playing with a Ouija board and explained that this had allowed demonic forces to enter their house. They repented of this and I came against the powers of darkness in Jesus' name and left. Later on they rang me to say that all the weird happenings had stopped. I was to experience many more such visits to homes in the years to come.

We were in Norwich for three years and we had to move on yet again. It was really hard because we had made good friends and seen a church develop from nothing. So much had been invested in the people and they stayed whilst we moved on.

We were so grateful to be given a little book of people's thanks to us and it meant a lot. Here are two very different comments:

"God has worked through you to touch people and change lives. God bless you richly for that."
"In your time here you have upset 3 Bishops, 1 Archdeacon, various clergy, assorted congregations, and lost a cup final. God knows what you would have achieved if you had been here longer!"

Pride of place in our loo is a framed gold disc of one of the children's songs that I wrote and that we sang – a lot!

So here we were, moving on for the fourth time in seven years. Our three eldest children were nearly 17, 14 and 12.

To complicate matters further Brandon refused to leave! He had friends there and was a member of a cricket and football team. He found a family to stay with and he got a job. With a heavy heart we had to leave him because he'd already been messed around too much. It was going to be a difficult time for Barney and Tammy and we were well aware of that.

I accepted the post of Vicar of Christ Church, Matchborough, in Redditch, near Birmingham, although I wasn't the first choice! It was June 1990 and I was about to find out that being a Vicar wasn't easy!

## REFLECTIONS:

As you can imagine one of the hardest things for us was to be constantly on the move. It had been the story of my childhood and now it was repeated in my job. It is so good that we have a close family and that all our children know that they are loved because moving as often as we did caused a lot of problems. Charm and I have moved over a dozen times in our married life.

It's a lonely life in the ministry and most people don't realize that. Your job title puts you in a different place in most people's eyes, and it's difficult to make close friends for fear of others thinking you've got a little clique around you.

Not having your own house is difficult too, especially with a family. We'd made our little house in Watford a home but that was long gone and we'd lost a lot of money on our decision to move. House prices shot up in the south and fell in Nottingham! We kept renting it out to families going to the Bible college but it became a noose around our neck with the upkeep and by the time we sold it we had little money to buy anything else. This was a source of pain and some unrest. If anything happened to me then Charm would be homeless.

One of the greatest thrills of my life is to be part of making God real to people. It's a tremendous privilege to see someone far from God have their eyes opened to their need of Him, along with a growing realization of His very real presence. It's literally seeing someone step out of darkness into light and then seeing their life change for the better. It's a miracle! I saw it a lot in Norfolk. The best way to show you this is to quote from a letter I received from one of the men in that group in my curacy:

"I have never told you what effect you had on my life. I praise God for your boldness when we first met, how you shared about Jesus with me and showed me that He was alive and loved me. If you had not challenged me I would not have known Him, His hope, His love."

Another man from our Norwich days wrote:

"You showed me where the door was and told me what lay beyond. I opened the door, let Jesus in, and He changed my life and that of my family."

Such words are so precious, so special, and remind me of why I went into the ministry.

Our seven years of training had been difficult, sometimes almost unbearable, but it was training for what was to come. Whenever anyone says to me that being a Vicar is easy I just about resist the desire to throttle them! They have no idea! People have this notion that you work on Sundays and do the occasional wedding, funeral and baptism and that's it! The next chapter will definitely put you straight!

Jesus told His first disciples that following Him would be tough and that many would fall away. He promised life in all its fullness but He said that the journey would not be easy. Why is this?

If we could pull aside the veil around us we'd see that there's a battle going on, a battle for every life. Jesus knew that battle as soon as He started His ministry on earth. Satan and his forces were constantly out to trip Him up and stop Him from fulfilling His destiny, which was to be the Saviour of the world. Right to the end they tried to stop Him from going to the Cross, because on the Cross Jesus paid the price for all of our sin, and in His resurrection He defeated the hold of death.

Jesus was, and is, God's only answer to our sin problem. Religion is mankind's attempt to know and please God whilst the essence of Christianity is about God coming to us and opening the way for a relationship with Him.

The result of all this is that Satan doesn't want anyone to know about Jesus and why He really came. He loves religion where people are tied up with rules and regulations, but he hates anyone realizing that it's about God's grace, about receiving God's offer of forgiveness through Jesus.

Whether I liked it or not, I, along with Charm and the family, were targets of the enemy's hatred. In the early days we didn't realize that, and even when you do realize it's not easy as you'll find out. I wanted to do everything I could to bring the reality of Jesus to people and their need of Him but as you've already seen there was a huge price to pay.

Over the next few years the cost at times would be difficult to bear.

**Chapter Five:**

## WHO SAID BEING A VICAR WAS EASY?
### (1990 – 2009)

My licensing service was in July 1990 and it was memorable because Charm got lost and was late! I preached on the Great Commission of Jesus from Matthew Chapter 28 and everyone seemed very happy. Some weren't so happy afterwards when I dared to change the chairs around! The decision was based on trying to make people feel more like a body of people. We had the width to do this and so there could be more eye contact. Even though it was a modern building traditions had set in!

My first Sunday service was memorable because I was involved in praying for deliverance for a young woman! I should have realized that things were going to get worse!

Christ Church, Matchborough, in Redditch is in the middle of two estates. Redditch itself is now a town of about 100,000 people and a lot of them come from Birmingham. Our estates had private housing on the outside and mainly council housing in the centre. The closer you get to the centre the more it becomes like a rabbit warren – you can easily get lost!

The people had done really well to raise money for a new building. It has a main area that can seat up to 250 people, with a baptistry under the carpet. There is a stage at one end, an office, a welcoming area with disabled facilities and a kitchen. Downstairs there are toilets, storage areas and a prayer room. It was designed to be a community church and it felt warm and inviting.

In the early days we had a lot of vandalism. The church is on a bus lane that is closed to other traffic so at night it is a haven for the local youth, especially with the shops opposite where they can buy drink. I would regularly have to go down in the middle of the night. On one occasion the police called me because a drug addict had crashed his way through one of the windows. Eventually we had to learn from the shopkeepers who had shutters and bars. This saddened us but the damage was extensive and prolonged. We have had some serious prayer into the vandalism and we often prayed around the building and in the shopping centre and we saw some positive results, but God also expected us to use common sense. There were a lot of empty units in the centre and it looked rundown. Some of us regularly prayer-walked around the centre, asking God to restore it. We were so thrilled when the day came that all the units were taken up!

My immediate observation was that the people had united behind getting a building but now that it was built there was no real unity of purpose. My task was to build up a body of people to be Christ's disciples. Sounds easy doesn't it?

It was clear that there were quite a few dominant people, controlling people. I came head to head with them early on. I'd only preached about becoming disciples and reaching out to others, as well as changing some chairs around, but almost half of the church council left! When I felt it right to dispense with our song and prayer books and sing from the overhead projector (with the council's backing) that was the last straw for others! I explained that we were still singing the same hymns and songs and saying the same prayers but they were now on a screen. It was no good to some! I explained that we lived in an area where people were not bookish and we needed to make them feel at home. I explained that without books we could all lift up our heads and worship God. It was no good to some and they left!

I remembered the words of my former college principal, Michael Green, who told me that when you went to a new place and preached the Gospel then half the congregation would leave before it built up again. I didn't believe him then but I did now!  It was a difficult time.  There was a youth group that wanted to be apart from the rest of the church and it had leaders who were very liberal in their views.  I had to confront this and so we lost the youth and the leaders!

I set about systematically teaching from the Bible.  I believe the Bible to be God's inspired Word for every generation and I believed that God would honour those who honoured Him.  I just didn't realize that it would take so long!

Christ Church is part of a team ministry that covers the east side of Redditch, about 30,000 people.  There were two other full-time vicars and we met weekly for prayer and business.  Getting together with other clergy became interesting!  There is what is called a chapter of clergy, like a gaggle of geese, and this met from time to time but I found it pretty turgid.  I wanted to find out if we had anything in common, and so I chaired a group of clergy from various denominations to discuss what we believed.  What emerged from this was that the majority just didn't have a belief that could unite us, and so I couldn't see the point in pretending that we did!

From this we hosted a meeting of those ministers who did have a faith in common and for a while it was good to pray together and share what was going on.  I felt we needed to action our unity and so we organized a united service, from which we would go out to circle Redditch in prayer.  It was really moving and quite a few people stopped their cars to ask us what we were doing.  We did this on another couple of occasions and it did unite us.

I was becoming really busy.  I found myself on the governing board of four schools at one point!  This was ridiculous so I made it two.  One of my fellow governors was Jacqui Smith, soon to become MP for Redditch, and at the time we were on first name terms.  My letters to her over the years have put an end to that!  I continued to be a governor at the

High School for about thirteen years and have seen three head teachers come and go. I also saw local policemen come and go and realised that an ongoing presence in the community was vital. Before me vicars had only stayed a few years and what was needed was commitment to the people and the area.

I went into the schools regularly to take assemblies. I wanted to make Jesus real to the pupils and so I took in my guitar and puppets! The great thing was that I became well-known in the neighbourhood and whenever I walked around there would be lots of "Hello, Rev Andy!" This still continues with the hellos coming from young people who remember me from school assemblies. I remember taking the Bishop of Worcester around the area on foot and he was amazed at the greetings as well as having his eyes opened to some of the problems.

We also have a fantastic Children's Nursery that uses our other building in the week. This used to be the where the church met and it has great facilities for youth and children's work. Quite a few of the Nursery staff are Christians and attend the church so there's been a great relationship. In the early days we had to pray hard to see things develop and prayer has always been at the heart of the work. The Nursery serves the community and is very well regarded having been described as outstanding by Ofsted. Again I would visit regularly and sing songs with them.

I had a desire to see the community more involved in the church and so I suggested that we put on a pantomime and invited people. Nobody thought it would work but I knew from previous experience that it would and so we embarked on a version of Treasure Island. I wrote the script before Christmas and we rehearsed from January until the February half-term, putting in four rehearsals a week! It was a great success and involved a lot of people, adults and children.

It also raised money for local schools and charities. Some people became Christians and joined the church and everybody wanted to do another one!

So the pantomime season went on for six years from 1993 to 1998. Each show became bigger and grander than before. We had so many people involved and a cast of over fifty. They were more like fully-blown musicals as there were about sixteen songs in each of them! I would rewrite well-known favourites like Robin Hood, Beauty and the Beast, and Snow White and we would rehearse really hard (four rehearsals a week for eight weeks)! The shows became so popular that one year we were forced to have a ten day run with 250 people a time! We even came to the notice of BBC Midlands Today who came to film us. It was a fantastic time and for those of us involved there will always be tremendous memories. Over the years hundreds of people got involved and many friendships were formed and some people became Christians and are active members of the church. The Bishop of Worcester at the time was a great fan! We raised over £15,000 for the community and it put the church right at the heart of local life which was thrilling.

Why didn't it continue? Well for one thing, I was exhausted! I was planning, writing, producing and acting in each one and it took its toll. There was also an expectation that the next one would be bigger, grander, with more effects and I felt that we needed to call a halt. It was taking up a lot of time and there were other challenges to be met.

Something really important happened to me around that time. For a few years I had played in the annual clergy golf tournament for the diocese. It is played at a very fancy club near Oxford and it's a really hard course. On this particular year I had a nightmare of a round. I just went from bad to worse and then could hardly hit the ball. People around me got embarrassed and I had to give up. Now I'm a Yorkshireman and we don't give up so it was really painful to me. I had been humbled and humiliated and it hurt, but it was as if God was saying to me, "Let's start over again shall we?" I don't mean about playing golf, I mean about my ministry.

And so it was. It was a turning point for me and for the church. I went to a leaders' conference about vision and I realized that we didn't have a clearly defined vision. Not long after this the word Seeds was imprinted on my heart and from this God's vision for the church was made clear. We had a large banner placed inside the church with the vision on it. It is there to this day and I hope will remain when I'm gone! This is what it says:

*Our vision at Christ Church is to be God's properly functioning body of disciples in line with the Acts 2 Church model so that Christ's saving purposes can be fulfilled in the world. This will be achieved through:*

*Submission Evangelism Embracing Discipleship Stewardship*
*We're SEEDS called to make Jesus known*

*Mission Statement: Enabling unbelievers to become disciples of Jesus Christ*
*Life Verse: 2Chronicles 7:14*

I began to teach the vision and encourage people to own it. We had cards made which you could put in your wallet or purse with the vision on them. This is what we stood for. This is where we were going. I was committed to seeing this vision become a reality.

I needed support because I realised we were in a spiritual battle for survival. There were a few faithful praying people in the church, but another area of support came from a most unexpected source. I was at a conference in the town and met

47

up with a pastor from Portugal who came from Angola. I invited him to the ministers group before he left and he gave out an invitation of his availability to help us. Nobody except me took him up and before long Charm and I found ourselves in Portugal! Afonso and his wife Elizabeth soon became our friends and we learned a lot from them. Their church was in a poor area and they really served the people. They took in young people and loved them and taught them how to serve. They fed people on the streets because there was no government support. They had been through really tough times and understood our battles.

And so they stood alongside us and we with them. Over the years they have stood back to back with us when things were difficult, sometimes coming over to speak to the leaders and the people. I cannot express how much I am indebted to them for their prayers and support. We have had some great times together over the last ten years, including walking through their town of Setubal in the early hours of the morning singing "Wait upon the Lord!"

Back in Redditch I had to keep going through steep learning curves. There was a spell when I was asked into people's homes because of demonic activity and I began to feel like a ghostbuster! People were frightened out of their wits and usually it was because they had dabbled in something which had allowed evil to enter. What was most amazing to me was that when the demonic activity stopped they didn't take Jesus seriously, even though it was obvious that His power had dispelled the evil.

Around this time there was quite a craze on TV evangelists and preachers. It's very easy to be taken in and as a church we were for a time. A fellow minister who I respected and who had taught in our church asked me to come to Wales to meet this "amazing woman of God." I went and found that she was amazing, larger than life in every sense. We warmed to her and she to us and the vision. I invited her to come and speak and she did. She seemed to have a hotline to God. She talked with people and prayed for people and they were captivated. She said that she felt everything around her so deeply that it affected her and she would shake and give prophetic words about what was going on.

Her main ministry had been in America but was now seen as worldwide. For a time I valued her teaching and input but there were some alarm bells. She started to insist on armour bearers which seemed like bodyguards and people in the church got drawn in. I became concerned about what authority she was under, and it appeared that she wasn't. It all came to a head when I disagreed about a particular issue and challenged her. I was really concerned about her effect on some of the people in the church. She didn't like being challenged and Charm and I bore the full brunt of her bodyguards when they told us that this was a mighty woman of God and we had better watch out! I don't like being threatened but the end result was very sad. We parted company and lost a few from the church. She had also been over to Afonso's church and caused some mayhem there, and this seemed to be the pattern.

People had been hurt and others deceived. We had some difficult leaders meetings at this time and to make matters worse we were hoodwinked by another charismatic preacher that we had all warmed to. We enjoyed his teaching and his books but then found out that he was womanizing and deceiving people. He was another one who was not under any authority and he did great damage.

There were hard lessons learned from all of this and I suppose it made me wary of "charismania." I was well aware of my responsibility to guard the people from wrong teaching and influences. I took the church through a variety of Bible based courses designed to encourage discipleship and the making of right choices and it all took time.

All of this turmoil affected the family of course and this is the cost of being a minister. Barney and Tammy had not had an easy time settling into new schools and they bore the stigma of being the vicar's children. Eventually Brandon joined us again so we were a full house! Our two youngest settled in well at first but as they got older they too endured the name-calling. Children can be very cruel.

The children in a clergy family hear and see everything. They saw how the hurt and criticism affected us and were aware of times when seeming friends let us down and overall they got a pretty jaundiced picture of church life. This saddens me so much and I have expressed this to each one of them, that although people let us down they must hold onto their faith in Jesus.

It wasn't all doom and gloom! We still had some great family holidays which they will always remember. The older children will always remember times in Wales with our friends Terry and Sheelagh and the fun we had on the beach! I used to get the better of Terry soaking him because I worked out the wind direction! Apart from Cornwall we also loved going to Sandsend, near Whitby in North Yorkshire. In the winter it could be quite wild with crashing waves and wonderful walks on the cliffs and the beach. Whitby itself is a quaint place with some of the best fish and chips in the world. We couldn't understand why people were queuing outside the Magpie Café by the quayside until we found out that this is where you were in for a treat!

My mother lived in North Yorkshire so it was good to see her when we visited. She had married again in her sixties to a Colonel and they were very happy. I got on much better with her, and we even took one of her dogs with us when she couldn't cope with it. At one point we had six dogs, most of them rescue dogs!

Although my mother wasn't very maternal she was quite a character! In her golfing days when women were frowned upon at the club she took on the men's captain who had boasted that men were far superior at golf. She humiliated him because she said that she would only use a putter the whole way round! Mark you in those days putters were like mallets. Needless to say she won and went down in local folklore! She was also always opening rights of way with her cutters much to the infuriation of the local farmers!

We also had great holidays in France camping with Eurocamp. The journey down to the South was a nightmare but once there it was fantastic. We went quite a few times and once we experienced a flash flood. It was amazing! One minute we were getting ready to eat and the next minute water was everywhere. Some Germans opposite us started to build a trench!

In 1997 Charm and I went to Kenya for our 25th Wedding Anniversary. It was a truly memorable time. We went on safari and saw some wonderful animals. One evening we were driven down to a swollen river and told to get into the dinghy with our case! A young lad rowed us across with difficulty and we found out it had crocodiles in it! When we arrived at the other side there was a hyena standing there! We camped that night and were told to zip our tent up tight! We went snorkelling off Zanzibar and the colours of the fish were breathtaking. We learned to windsurf and on the one wet day we learned to scuba dive! We only intended to learn in the pool but the next minute we found ourselves out in a boat doing a dive! Charm hung onto the instructor for dear life!

In Kenya you barter for everything and I enjoyed doing that. We got friendly with a local taxi driver who was a Christian.

He took us to see his mother but there was a language barrier as she spoke no English! On our last day he appeared with a big crate of fruit that he wanted us to take back! It would have cost us the earth in excess luggage! We were greatly moved by the poverty and yet the people seemed so happy and the generosity was amazing. We became good friends with the barman, Charles, who fixed us lovely cocktails! He worked all hours for a pittance and when we returned to England we decided to support him and his family, so that his children could go to school. Tragically his eldest daughter got raped and murdered just before going to university. It's a violent place. We're now trying to help his son, Joel, through medical school.

We also enjoyed family holidays with the younger ones in Turkey. I was offered camels for Charm and Kimberley but had to decline as I couldn't get them on the plane! We went to Ephesus where St. Paul had started a church and we went to the hot springs nearby which are great to bathe in. We also had a mud bath and a real Turkish massage! The people were friendly and I had lots of conversations with them about faith. They told me that they liked me and our family but if I came and started a church there then they would kill me! My eyes were opened to the violent spirit in Islam.

A great thrill for me was a day at Silverstone which Charm gave me as a present for my 50th birthday. I drove a Formula First around the track and it was speedy! I didn't realize how speedy until I got back in my car and driving on the motorway seemed like a crawl!

Back in Redditch let me just chart our children's fortunes. We prayed Brandon through his paramedic exams but after a few years he resigned for various reasons and retrained as a driving instructor and during this time married Penny. Barney had been to university and paid for the good time like all students with debts, and eventually joined the police. Tammy left school to join Specsavers where she eventually became a manager. She is engaged to Brad and they are both keen rugby fans! Brandon and Penny presented us with our first grandchild Joshua and eighteen months later with our second, Joseph. Barney got married to Amanda, and it was at the same church in Cornwall where Charm and I had wed. Kim left school and joined the catering trade eventually becoming assistant manager at a local restaurant where she became engaged to the chef, Antony. With such unsocial hours and pressures she eventually left and is now working in sales. Beth left school to go to university to study nursing, which she didn't enjoy. Sensibly, she left, got a job and re-took an A level and has returned to university to study English, which she really does enjoy. She has been elected onto the Christian Union committee and is really excited about the possibilities. It's wonderful to see her grow in her faith walk. I'm so proud of them all and love them so very much!

Charm had been working as a district nurse for nearly ten years and then got a job as a Marie Curie Nurse Specialist in Solihull, Birmingham. After four years there she moved to a palliative post in Evesham and Worcester. This work is very demanding and draining and takes its toll. Charm had to have some time out in 2003 and I'm sure she'll tell you about it in the next chapter. From time to time she asks me to see a patient who requests this and it has always been very humbling.

I will always remember James, a young man in his early twenties with everything to live for who developed terminal cancer. He had a lot of questions and I tried to answer some of them. Before he died he gave his life to Jesus and he was an inspiration to his family and friends. I also remember Patricia who was 49. She and her husband Graham battled this cancer and prayed and sought God with all their heart but she died. I was privileged to know them for a while and their situation underlined the fact that there are so many unanswered questions this side of eternity.

In 2004 I got completely worn out and then depression struck again. I just came shuddering to a halt. Things had taken their toll. I was off work for three months and didn't want to see anybody. I went on a course of anti-depressants which I've now been on for over four years. I tried to write in a journal and read books that would help me draw closer to God. I'd also been diagnosed with an under active thyroid, irritable bowel syndrome, and a hiatus hernia which didn't help. The hernia investigation meant a camera down the throat! Until then I was someone who ate pills because I couldn't swallow them! I really prayed about it and amazingly I swallowed the camera without too much fuss. Now I can swallow horse pills! The thyroid problem meant some weight gain and tiredness so all-in-all it wasn't a good time.

I returned to work at Christmas and the church seemed genuinely pleased to see me. For my part I knew I had to slow down and that wasn't going to be easy. One area of ministry that had really taken off was writing to the press. I felt so grieved about the erosion of our Christian inheritance and couldn't remain silent. The Daily Mail has often printed my letters along with the local papers and the result has been lots of criticism! Sadly, hardly any of the other local ministers were willing to put themselves in print and the result has been over the years that I am targeted. There will be some people in Redditch who will be very pleased to see me go!

The result of my writing in the media has also led to some great opportunities. I have had many radio interviews and some television coverage. My interview on Radio Four's "Today" programme led to much media interest. It was concerning the British Airways official who was suspended for wearing a cross. Little did the public know but the taxi taking me to the studio was late, so I was run along the corridor, shoved into a studio, had earphones banged on my head and told "You're on!" Fortunately it went well!

I think I got this letter-writing thing from my mother and it really pleased her to know that I was getting into the press. My letters column on our website has caused a lot of interest. It's costly too and you have to have broad shoulders.

I have always tried to avoid personal comments but unfortunately my critics have not. The result is that I have been pilloried, slandered, castigated and hung out to dry! Sometimes it takes its toll but the alternative is to remain silent and I just can't do that.

On the church front we were at last seeing some fruit! We had employed a Community Worker, Phil, an ex-head teacher, and this resulted in the church being used by the community in the week as we teamed up with the local college to host courses. We started an older people's lunch and activities club and the place was (and still is) buzzing all week! Church members became involved to help and there was real teamwork. Eventually the Community Project got the recognition that it deserved and it gained charity status which means that we have been able to obtain various grants to improve both community and youth activities.

Our links with Portugal saw our youth group grow and develop incredibly. At one point we had very few young people and no actual youth group. A few of us met regularly for months on a Friday night to pray. We cried out to God, made ourselves available, and asked that a new work would start. In time it did and then grew and grew! Some good leaders came forward but we were at the mercy of youth culture. They had no idea how much they had, how much they took for granted.

So one half-term we sent them to Portugal! Sounds good doesn't it? But this wasn't the Algarve, it was Setubal, the streets, and a gipsy settlement where few dared to go! We wanted them to learn how to serve and they did! They served meals on the streets, picked up rubbish, and went to the gipsy area where only Afonso was really welcome because of the care his church had shown them. Here they helped and had their eyes opened. When they returned they were a very different group and the effects of the trip lasted. Many of them got baptized and they had grown up. The next year we sent them again but this time they took a programme of drama, dance and music with them, much of which they performed in the open. They all benefited hugely from the experience and having visited an orphanage they were keen the following year to invite some of these youngsters over to Redditch.

The result was that we had a camp, just outside Redditch, with our young people, and youngsters from the orphanage along with their Catholic priest. It was a fantastic time. The Mayor of Setubal and another council leader came over to see what was going on and they were so impressed at how our young people were looking after everyone.

We have a tremendous group of young people now, who are committed to God and to each other and want to reach out to their generation. Our leaders have been fantastic and we have been greatly encouraged to have Afonso's eldest son, Daniel, join us to work with the young people while studying for a degree. I am reminded of those days when we had no youth and we prayed from our hearts that God would start a new work. Everything of worth in the church has come about as people have really prayed and sought God. It's a key lesson that is all too easy to forget. In 2007 I was sixty and we had a fantastic weekend! Invitations were sent out for a 1960's disco/fancy dress party and people really responded. My good friend Ian and I supplied the cabaret! He's a great singer who now tours everywhere with his Neil Diamond tribute act, and I did my Elvis thing! Family came from Cornwall and elsewhere and it was a memorable night. I challenged the church people to come in their fancy dress to the service next day and many did, including Charm and myself! The funny thing was that some people came to hear banns of marriage read who had never been before so they got quite a shock!

Christ Church has always been good at parties. The building lends itself to any occasion which is great. It can be a worship area, a restaurant, a theatre, a workshop area, a lecture area, or a keep-fit area! It's very multi-purpose.

A great surprise for my 60$^{th}$ birthday was to go on a skiing holiday with some of the family. I hadn't skied for over forty years and then I was hurtling down the mountain as a fearless teenager! But I loved it! We went to Austria and it was a picture-postcard place with beautiful chalets and awesome mountains. Charm had a traumatic week trying to learn but she didn't give up and wanted to return. I found that it all came back to me after the first day and I loved it.

After twenty three years in the ministry I finally took a sabbatical and decided to write a book. It's called "Too many questions, not enough answers, or are there?" Over the years I've been asked so many questions and I wanted to put some of the answers in a format that people could understand. The book covers topics such as:

1. Why you can trust the Bible.
2. Science and the Bible.
3. Sickness, suffering and pain.
4. Sin, death, heaven and hell.
5. Religions and cults.

I'm thrilled that many people have been helped by the book and some have come to faith. It was a joy to dedicate it not only to the family but to the memory of James and Patricia who I mentioned earlier.

The church survived whilst I was away and that was good! We have seen some good leaders emerge over the years and this is vital for a church's growth. The one area where we were lacking was in worship. We have some talented musicians but I had been leading worship all the time I had been there. I needed someone to take this role and it's not easy but it's so important. When the young people decided that they would lead a service once a month I was so thrilled to see them engage in singing and playing instruments. Now we are integrating all ages into the worship team and some have volunteered to take on a leadership role.

Over the years I have written a lot of songs for worship services and we are going to be putting together two CD's before I leave – one of children's songs and one of praise and worship songs. Hopefully they will be a good resource for the church and something to remember us by!

+     +     +

One of my great loves is rugby and Charm and I have been season ticket holders at Worcester Warriors for a few years, seeing them come up into the premiership. I contacted the director of rugby at Worcester offering any help and at the same time he was contacted by the Rugby Union Chaplaincy in Sport coordinator asking about the possibility of having a chaplain at the club. We all met up and I was asked to take on the role of Chaplain at Worcester Warriors! It was pretty daunting. As you can imagine a rugby club is quite a macho environment and a chaplain will sink or swim quickly! Premiership rugby clubs are big concerns now. Not only are there the first team squad and the academy players on the books but also a whole host of staff so that you are talking about a hundred people or more. My task was to make myself known and to be available to whoever needed me, and I've tried to do that. It's a very friendly club and I have been made very welcome. Some of the players who are Christians like to meet up with me regularly and some of them are from the South Sea Islands. I asked one of them from Fiji why so many players from there were Christians. He told me it was because of our missionaries. First of all they ate them, and then they took them seriously!

Professional sport can be short-lived because of injury and there are lots of pressures on the players and staff. I believe I serve a useful purpose by being around to listen, to encourage, and, where needed, to pray and give some answers when asked. I was thrilled to be asked to write a regular piece in the matchday programmes. I try to get my point across around a story because everyone likes stories. Worcester Warriors has a great sense of family about it and the fans have been very loyal. I love the role and I so want the club to do well. For too many seasons we're scrabbling down the bottom of the league and it's not good for blood pressure and finger nails!

One summer the Team Rector went on holiday and never returned. He had a heart attack and died. It was really sad. The problem in the Church of England is that if the minister dies then the widow has to vacate the vicarage pretty quickly. Charm and I had been aware of this and we had managed to buy a little place in Whitby. It was lovely but a long way to go to look after it. We realized that our family was all in the Midlands area and we needed to find somewhere nearer. We were fortunate for once that house prices rose and when my Mother died we were able to buy a house in the country near Evesham.

My mother had come to live near Northampton being much more frail now and it meant that my brother could keep an eye on her. I visited her quite regularly but she started to need more care. She had always been such a fiercely independent lady and she hated getting old. The last straw for her was to have to go into a home and she died there. There was sadness to the last because she had left most of what she had to my brother. I don't know why but he very graciously persuaded her that this was not right and so the will was changed. It's a good job or else we'd be homeless!

After nearly twenty years as Vicar of Christ Church I am starting to see the vision become a reality! When I started out I felt like Joshua having to take the people forward into new territory. Now I feel like Moses who has to pass the baton on to someone else. It's the right time to go, sad as it will be. The church needs God's new leader who will enable the vision to flourish. It will be such a great place for the new vicar to come to! Years ago, at our worst point, I wondered whether things would ever really change. But they have, and there are great structures in place and excellent leaders. We have a couple of fantastic Church Wardens in John and Joan. Joan has been my secretary over all these years and I am indebted to her for her hard work, her support, her prayer, and her friendship. We have had a lot of banter over the fact that she is from Lancashire and I'm from Yorkshire! I have seen John grow into a wonderful leader, and the church is privileged to have him at the helm. One of the keys to leadership in the church is to make yourself redundant, and I believe that I have!

Michael Green was right! I lost nearly half the membership in those first few years as I set out to preach God's Word. Now, the membership has more than doubled and there is unity! It's taken me nearly twenty years and it has been costly, but I'm thrilled that we've come this far. Years ago I went to a conference called "That none should perish." This is my heart's desire, that everyone should come to know Jesus and then grow into maturity as disciples. This summer will be the last time that I visit homes in the area with other members of the church. We've been doing this every summer for some years, telling people that we're here for them and that we're praying for them. I hope that the church will continue to do this so that the people know that we care.

This Easter Sunday was the last time that I met with other Christians on the little hill above Morrisons at 7am to pray for the people of Redditch, which we have been doing for years. I hope that this will continue as well. Prayer and action should go together and I have always sought to do this. If you believe that Jesus really is the Way, the Truth, and the Life then you must try to reach people. It's the greatest thrill for me to be involved in communicating the truth of Jesus to someone and seeing that person respond. This Easter Sunday as always we had our Baptism service where a lot of people, young and old, went under the water! It's so thrilling when someone wants to make that public declaration of faith and it's so moving. My wife, Charm, was baptized as a teenager but didn't totally go under so she wanted to renew her baptism vows. I made sure she went under! Actually she was very brave because she was recovering from a broken ankle. She had a cast on and a special waterproof stocking. When she entered the water the stocking blew up like a balloon and we thought it was filling up with water! Fortunately it was air and she was all right.

On the family front we're thrilled that our daughter Tammy is going to get married in October to Brad. The wedding will be in Cornwall where we got married and I shall be taking the service as well as giving the bride away, which will be interesting! I shall also be singing a few Elvis songs in the evening as a cabaret! Brandon and Penny were expecting their third child in September which now turns out to be twins (!) and I think the number of grandchildren will increase over the next few years from other quarters of our family! Our Sunday family lunch gatherings will get bigger and bigger, but it's great! Eating together as a family is so important, which is why Charm and I so value these times as we do Christmas gatherings. It was lovely this year as we also had two of the Worcester Warrior players with us as their families were back in Fiji and New Zealand.

I've handed over the next two chapters to Charm and the family. It's really important that they give their insights into this journey, and hopefully this will be of real help to some of you reading this. They'll be honest; I can assure you of that!

## FINAL REFLECTIONS

There's so much to thank God for in our time at Christ Church, but as you've journeyed with me through this time you will know that there was a lot of pain too. I think that is inevitable if you want to see a vision become reality. I probably could have been a little wiser in my early years in Redditch and a bit more patient, and I'm truly sorry if I upset anyone unnecessarily.

Sadly I also came to realize that there are disaffected people in every church and the Church of the Disaffected would be the largest in the world if they all got together! I used to have a notepad with a picture of a man with a knife in his back. It read, "Thanks for your help!" I've had more than my share of those who've knifed me in the back, rubbished me, and criticized me, and I certainly won't miss that aspect of the ministry!

I've always been enthusiastic about Jesus and I've wanted to make church an exciting, challenging and fun place to be, because I believe the Church is the hope of the world, and therefore I believe that the local church is the hope of that community. Why do I say that? I'm well aware of the problems in the Church but when someone gives their life to Jesus they become part of His body on earth. That is awesome! A Christian is called to be salt and light and needs to be part of a worshipping community in order to grow. If the sole purpose of Jesus' mission was to save people then when they were saved He'd take them straight to Heaven! But Jesus has chosen to work through His people, even though we often mess it up. When the Church functions properly it is the greatest sign of God's presence in the world. I meet people who say that they don't need to go to church to be a Christian. Wrong comment! If you're a Christian then you are part of the church.

People have such a wrong image of Jesus and the Church hasn't helped. Every time I take a wedding I remind people that Jesus' first miracle was at a wedding reception when the wine ran out. It was seriously embarrassing for the couple's parents, but Jesus stepped in and saved the day. And what a party ensued! There were over six hundred litres of the very best wine! That is not the action of a party-pooper! I tell people that Jesus offers them forgiveness of sin, a relationship with God, life everlasting, hope, joy, peace, purpose, and that you'll never find these things on offer at Tesco, and you'll never get them by winning the lottery! Jesus is unique.

The problem with the Church is that for too long it's preached the wrong message. There's no point telling people about Jesus until they realize why they need Him. Jesus came to be our Saviour because we need saving. Without Jesus, God will judge us by the laws He gave to Moses, which we call the Ten Commandments. Sadly, most people have no idea what they are now.

Whenever I know that there are quite a few non-Christians in the church then I take them through some of the commandments. Let me show you:

Have you ever told a lie? That makes you a liar, and you've broken the ninth commandment. (Politicians please take note!) Have you ever taken something, however small, that's not yours? That makes you a thief, and you've broken the eighth commandment. (Politicians please take note!)

Have you ever used the name God or Jesus to express anger or frustration? That makes you a blasphemer, and you've broken the third commandment.

Have you ever looked at someone with lust? That makes you an adulterer, and you've broken the seventh commandment.

Then I say "If you and I are honest, so far that makes us lying, thieving, blaspheming adulterers, and we've only looked at four commandments!" If people realize this then they know that they're in trouble before a holy God. They are much more likely then to want to hear about Jesus and how He came to pay the price for our sins.

Weddings are such fantastic occasions and there's a vital truth that needs to be expressed. Every wedding reminds us that Jesus is coming again for His bride. When the bridegroom stands at the front he represents Jesus, and when the bride walks down the aisle she represents the Bride of Christ. Who is this Bride? She is the Church, made up of everyone who has opened their heart to Jesus and recognized Him as their Saviour. I point this out to people and challenge them to become part of that Bride before it's too late.

Whenever you say something as a Vicar or have something in print then some people will misconstrue it. Some will only hear what they want to hear and others will misunderstand.

It can be really frustrating but that's life! I always have full notes of what I preach as well as recordings on CDs' so that if there are any problems I can refer to what was actually said. The problem is that often the damage is done as people talk to others about what they think I said! Classic examples come from my book, "Too many questions......."

It's said that I'm homophobic, Islamaphobic, and that someone who has cancer has sinned. None of these are true! On the issue of homosexuality, I have stated what the Bible teaches, but alongside that I have also stated that the Bible condemns sex outside of marriage. God loves each person but hates sin in whatever form. He knows what is best for us and the Bible is His manual for right living. When we don't heed God's advice then we reap the consequences, which sadly we see all around us. As a Bible teacher I would be failing my call if I did not make this clear without fear or favour. I believe with all my heart in God's grace and power. His grace loves each person unconditionally and His power can enable people to become who He created us to be. I hope that I respond to people as Jesus did. To Him it didn't so much matter where they had been or what they had done. What mattered to Jesus was where they were going. Anyone, anywhere, can be transformed into a new person through the grace and power of God.

On the issue of Islam, I have stated facts about its beginnings and about the teaching of the Koran. Most people have no idea that 1 out of every 55 verses in the Koran is a war verse, intended to arouse Muslims to compel the conversion of non-Muslims to Islam, by violence if necessary. If anyone refuses to acknowledge Mohammed as God's prophet, and the Koran as inspired by Allah, then you're an infidel and worthy of death. Now these are facts and people need to know them and I have a responsibility to make them known. If a person dares to come out of Islam and wants to become a Christian then they are persecuted and often killed. I have firsthand experience of this. I am well aware that there are lots of moderate Muslims who want to be law-abiding and peaceful but the fact is that the extremists, as they are called, are the ones being faithful to the teaching of the Koran. I have no hatred of Muslims, or of gay people. On the contrary, I want them to know the freedom and love that is found in Jesus Christ.

With regard to cancer and sin I have never said that a person with cancer has it as a result of some sin in their life. That would be a cruel and false thing to say. What I have said is what the Bible teaches, that cancer is the result, as are all other diseases, of ongoing genetic deterioration in our body cells because of the Fall, the consequence of mankind's rebellion against God. In the beginning God created a perfect world and man and woman lived in it without suffering or disease, but when they rebelled against God then death, disease and suffering entered our world and we all inherit these things. On the Cross Jesus paid the price for our sins and one day when He returns there will be no more death, disease or misery. It will be life as God originally intended, which is why we need to make sure that Jesus is our Saviour. If any of my critics are reading this then I hope that gives you an answer.

Our links with Portugal have been so vital for our growth and our survival. Back in 1999 Afonso and I made a covenant to always be there for each other. A covenant in the Bible is awesome and it means that whatever happens to you happens to them. You are so closely linked in both good and bad times. This has proved to be true. Now my friend Afonso is a Bishop which means that I'm a Bishop too! I don't think the Church of England will be too happy about this! He is heavily engaged in Angola where he was born, trying to bring God's love in action to that war-torn country. We are privileged to be involved, in helping to support programmes that will see the building of homes and schools and hospitals and shops and agriculture. Our young people are keen to get behind this project which is wonderful to see.

When we came to Christ Church our youngest, Beth, was just two. Now she is twenty one. We have seen a whole generation of children grow into early adulthood and it's been a wonderful part of our journey. I've baptized them and I've taken their weddings and that's special! I've been involved in people's grief and loss on so many occasions and it's always humbling. Now we have to part company and it won't be easy.

Charm and I will so miss the Christmas and Easter services. They've always been special at Christ Church and many of the community come along year after year. The variety is what we love. The Christingle service is a lot of fun with lots of groups taking part, including the Nursery with their nativity play. The key moment is when we circle the inside of the church with the candles in the oranges and turn the lights out. It's really moving. Our Carols by Candlelight is attended by those who have lost loved ones in the year and so it is very poignant. Our Midnight service is by candlelight and it's such a wonderful start to Christmas Day. On Christmas Day we have a short service that is a lot of fun with balloons and party poppers and songs. Great!

Easter for us starts with our Passover meal on Maundy Thursday. A lot of people come. We sit on the floor around low tables and we re-enact some aspects of that Last Supper that Jesus had with His disciples. It's very moving. On Good Friday we have Time at the Cross from 12 noon until 3 pm. It's a time to reflect on what Jesus did for us, as we listen to the story unfold, along with the prophecies that Jesus fulfilled. It's a really powerful time. On Easter Day some of us are up early overlooking Redditch where we sing and where we pray for the people. At our main service we celebrate Jesus' resurrection and we have Baptisms by immersion and Renewal of Baptism vows. It's fantastic!

When you enter Christ Church you can't help noticing an enormous Cross. It's freestanding on a base and it's a reminder to us of who and what unites us. At every service, just after the time of confession, there is an opportunity to come up to the Cross to kneel and reflect on God's saving love. We also use this time as an occasion to give our tithes and offerings as an act of humble worship at the Cross and it's powerful. Our giving ought to be worshipful and sacrificial, not giving God our leftovers. God has certainly honoured this response over the years.

I hope by now you'll have realised that being a Vicar isn't easy but just in case I'll spell it out! In order to do the job properly a Vicar needs to be able to preach and teach God's Word, be a shepherd, a counsellor, and a visionary. He needs to be available at all times and needs to lead by example. He needs to be an encourager, a motivator, a pioneer. He needs to proclaim God's Truth without fear or favour, but tempered with grace and love. He needs to have a heart for the people and their development, enabling others' gifts to flourish. He needs to have God's concern for those who do not yet know Christ. He needs wisdom and discernment to lead and protect God's people. He needs to have a deep and growing relationship with God, broad shoulders and he needs a sense of humour! He is greatly helped if he has the support of a wife!

Now it's Charm's turn to put the record straight!

# Chapter Six:
## CHARM'S CHAPTER

In case anyone's wondering my proper name is Charmian (pronounced as Sh, it just gets shortened to Charm!) Andy and I discussed the writing of this book a few years ago, partly in response to several people who on hearing bits of our experiences told us we should really be putting it in writing. Some months ago, knowing we were approaching the end of our time in parish ministry, he decided it was time to put pen to paper - and got on and did it! This is the way he always is. If he decides something needs to be done he does it! I, on the other hand, think about it, get sidetracked, and generally put things off! I think procrastination is one of my greatest – I was going to say gifts – it's hardly that! It's probably a weakness rather than a strength but it's part of who I am, a bit of a 'last minute' person! At least now I have started as Magnus Magnusson used to say on Mastermind, 'so I will finish!'

## BACKGROUND

I developed a love of English Literature thanks to an inspirational teacher when I was doing my A Levels back in 1966-8. 'The Child is father of the Man' is a line from Wordsworth which for some reason resonated with me as a teenager, and came to mind as I was mulling over how to start and what to say. Experience has convinced me that the majority of people recognize an inner core of their being which has always been present, from childhood, through adulthood to old age, an essential ageless something which gives each of us our unique identity. An element of the child we once were remains with all of us and certain aspects of our characters, and ways of thinking, although obviously developed over the years, I believe we will probably find can be traced back to our childhood. One of the 'constants' in my life has been a love of nature, both as an observer and as a gardener. When I think back this was doubtless initiated in me by both my father and my stepmother (I hate that word)! I remember my Dad pointing out beautiful views to me, (I'm not sure how much I actually appreciated them at the time), sharing with me the wonders of the night sky, and allowing me to stay up late to see a hedgehog eating from a saucer from the back door. As a small girl I remember my stepmother growing lovely flowers and arranging them beautifully in vases. She also nurtured in me a love of birds and I remember making a messy bird cake with a recipe from an Enid Blyton book! The family have learnt to be indulgent of Mum's need to feed and water the birds. Watching wildlife in the garden continues to give me great pleasure.

However, as a teenager my greatest love in nature was the sea, which since I am Cornish and grew up in Cornwall is not surprising, and it is a love affair which continues to this day. I would spend hours walking by the sea, swimming in it or simply gazing at it, sometimes alone, often with a good school friend. I had been brought up to go to Sunday-school and Church but had no real personal faith or understanding of the Gospel. However, I would look at the sea and just know that there had to be a Creator of this amazing ever-changing beauty which seemed to stretch to infinity. Like most teenage girls, I imagine, I would also think of the man I would one day fall in love with. I always felt, almost **knew,** that some day I would meet the right man and that I would know without any doubt that this was the only one for me. This did not prevent me from 'fancying' boys or having several boyfriends! One in particular I must have gone out with for almost three years and was very fond of. However, I remember being quite horrified when he commented that he thought most of the couples in our group of friends would one day marry! I knew that, much as I liked him, there was no way I would marry him. It was during those years, and partly through this boyfriend, that I became a Christian when I was fourteen. I attended a Baptist Church and received excellent Biblical teaching, which helped me greatly through college years. We were a very active youth group, holding coffee bars where we would go out on the streets 'fishing' for young people to invite back for coffee and chat and the opportunity to watch 'Fact and Faith' films. We also went to many different churches to give our testimonies. This together with my years at University meant that I had had some experience of most denominations by the age of twenty-one! I knew that 'denomination' was a man-made irrelevance. What was/is important is a person's relationship with Jesus Christ. However, I digress!

On completion of my A Levels my plan was to go to Sheffield University to study psychology with a view to becoming a clinical psychologist. I was sensing the desire to do something 'medical', had done the wrong A Levels for Medicine to be an option, and didn't even consider Nursing. The view of my school was that to become a nurse was a waste of our education! However, in spite of a predicted B I failed French, like Andy, but unlike him I hadn't been to school in Switzerland! I was disappointed, but as a Christian accepted that God had other plans for me. I would have liked to have taken a gap year, but that was frowned on so I ended up going through the 'Clearing' Scheme and being accepted to do an English degree in London. As we queued for our grants all our conversations were about where we had wanted to go, what we had wanted to study and which subject we had failed. Not the most auspicious of starts and the buildings weren't exactly full of character!

Undaunted I was determined to make the best of it, joined the hockey team, and became very involved in the Christian

Union. Although I was clear in my mind that it would be wrong to marry a non-Christian that did not prevent me from dating non- Christians. After all I **knew** that somewhere was my one and only, and he would have to be a Christian. Even though it was the early 70's, and of course there were those who indulged in casual sex, I never felt any pressure to enter into a sexual relationship and, in spite of the popular impression of the time; it was not necessarily the 'norm' to do so. My first year came and went with holidays spent at home in Cornwall working as a chambermaid in various hotels.

## BEGINNINGS

It was during that year that I first saw Andy, watching a rugby international as he has described. For me, if it wasn't love at first sight, it came close! We were subsequently introduced by our mutual friend John. Andy and I were two of very few in the Hall of Residence who were studying English so that gave us an automatic link. I would often be invited to his room for coffee. He had a percolator, which was considered a luxury! We often had debates about Christianity but equally often he would withdraw into himself and we would sit in silence for ages with me not knowing what to say. I was a bit frightened of him in those days! What a difference to now when we so easily spend time in companionable silence simply appreciating each other's presence. I of course in these early days had no idea of the depth of the hurt he had experienced, nor the pain it had caused him, nor the fear and distrust he had of any future relationship. Even if I had it would have made no difference to the way I was feeling! Suddenly I, who had been so black and white in my views about what was right, felt totally out of control. Initially the relationship was totally platonic but gradually things developed and I discovered a new side to myself! I became aware that given the opportunity I would have been willing to sleep with

Andy. I knew this was wrong and even read a book to work out if I could be forgiven if I did! This little book talked about the sin of presumption, which answered my question and fortunately for me at that time it didn't become an option!

However, I knew I was hopelessly in love and didn't know how to cope. I remember one evening coming back from his room and banging my fist against my bedroom wall and shouting 'Lord, I love him. I don't know what to do'. Also around this time when we were having coffee the realization flashed through my mind that I never wanted to have children with anyone but him. Until that moment I hadn't thought of having children at all! Spiritually there was a battle going on as I was avoiding Christian friends and church.

Back in Cornwall at Easter I went to my home church and just by being there was challenged by the claims of Christ on my life. I remember afterwards sitting on the cliffs and praying. I knew I had to put God first and that meant telling Andy it was over. There are no words to describe how awful I felt, but I knew I had to make the 'right choice'. Ironic that many years later that phrase would become so well known through Andy's preaching! He has described my return to London, and his response floored me totally! I had been so determined to break off all contact and now he was telling me that he wouldn't have come back if I hadn't been there. I went back to my room and read 1 John, (all about Christian love) and asked God to show me how to show 'Christian' love without compromising my decision. You have read Andy's account. I have always wondered, if I had made my 'right choice' sooner would he have accepted Christ sooner and saved us both some difficult months? Obviously I was thrilled, but this was the beginning, not the end! I knew about the difficulties of Andy's past but naively assumed that now he had found Christ and had me to love him all the problems resulting from his hurts would be resolved. I was young and had yet to learn that both the healing of deep emotional hurts and the development of spiritual maturity is a long process, not an instant fix.

We married in September 1972 and looking back it's amazing that we survived the first few years. My father's sudden death only three weeks after our wedding was terrible for me, I loved him very much. He had played an enormous part in my childhood, nurturing in me, apart from other things, a great love of sport. My real mother died when I was only five and he, together with my aunt and 'Ruth' who was to become my stepmother (awful word) and who I called Mum from early days, protected me from a lot of the pain and distress of that time. Losing Dad at that time so unexpectedly, (he was only fifty one) was devastating to me and left me with many regrets. I was also so sad for Mum who was ten years younger than him and was left with three young children to bring up alone. I also felt useless as we lived so far away and had a lot of problems of our own!

Brandon arrived just eleven months after our wedding and I used to wash all his towelling nappies and baby clothes by hand! When he was only about six weeks old we had to move, first into someone's spare room and then to the freezing Victorian house in Lewisham. We had also acquired two border collie puppies just prior to Brandon's birth! We have been prone to making impetuous decisions at times! However, our pets have always been an integral part of our family. Fortunately, Mum had had twins when I was eleven and another baby when I was seventeen, and I had always loved babies so looking after Brandon came very naturally to me. This was just as well given our circumstances! We'd actually lived in seven different places before we got our own home in Watford when Brandon was just over a year old! This included three weeks in a small caravan in the Vicar's garden in Wealdstone until a room became available in their house. It was cold! How we ever managed to get ourselves dressed respectably enough to go to our teaching jobs I'll never know!

It was so special to move into our own home and we set to, decorating and putting our own stamp on it. Having got the necessary mortgage I immediately reduced my hours to halftime, which I continued until Barnaby was born in December 1975. We had very few possessions, and initially everything was second hand. We never really had enough money but survived somehow and remain grateful to Mum for providing many weeks of free holiday accommodation in Cornwall over the years! I had a variety of part-time jobs which included counting out wage packets for Laing the builders (a nightmare!) and trying to sell double glazing! The early years were difficult at times and I do remember once feeling fairly desperate, and that I was doing all the 'giving' in the relationship and I briefly considered running back to Cornwall! However my love for Andy never wavered and I knew we were meant to be together and gradually our relationship became stronger and stronger. It was so sad when I had a miscarriage on Christmas night in 1976 but we were thrilled when our first daughter Tammy arrived in December the following year. Sometimes good things can come out of loss!

I enjoyed being a young Mum and was involved in church activities, toddler groups, and playgroups. I became a teacher with the National Childbirth Trust and had a lot of friends. These were the days before working mothers were the norm and in spite of the lack of money I'm so glad I had those years at home. I started my Nurse Training in September 1981 a few months before Tammy's fourth birthday. I am glad I did it as it led eventually to my present job, although with hindsight I question whether it was right to do it at that time, although I don't think it adversely affected the children. We'll see what they say! My energy and stamina levels must have been high! Ten day stretches were the norm and I remember doing an eight week stretch of nights, eight on, seven off! I would get to bed at 09:30 hrs having walked Brandon Barney and Tammy the twenty minute walk to their school and back. I would have to be up again by 14:30 hrs to pick them up! That was following the first of what was to be far too many school moves for them. We had become increasingly unhappy with the school they were attending and had moved them not knowing that only twelve months later we would be moving to Nottingham. Andy was extremely supportive throughout this time and I certainly couldn't have managed it without him.

It was when I first started training that he had the serious depression that he has spoken about. It was a learning curve for both of us and I just tried to be supportive and love him through it. For his own part he showed great strength of character in battling it, making himself do things and also being willing to help other people we met at that time who were struggling. He was referred to a psychiatrist who he found totally unhelpful. I know he spent time crying out to God. He returned to teaching the following term, in my opinion largely through sheer will power and a determination to trust God to get him through. The call to the ministry and subsequent outworking, like many things in our lives, happened very quickly. I think I felt it was right for him, but personally I didn't really fancy the idea of being a Vicar's wife! Deep down I think I probably sensed that the move would involve a lot of losses - especially the sense of security and stability and the circle of good friends we had. It's a good job we cannot see into the future – if I knew all that lay ahead I definitely would have wanted to stay put!

## MOVING ON

Although sad to leave our home in Watford and concerned for the children (now 10, 7 and 5) for me the two years in Nottingham were happy. I completed my training and then worked three nights a week as a Staff Nurse. I didn't actually enjoy nights at all but thought it would be less disruptive, and it was a bit more money for less hours! St John's College was family orientated and I was able to attend quite a few sessions there. No-one was there for long so we were all in the same boat of everything being temporary. However when I picked Tammy up on her last day at school she sat in the car beside me and said nothing but tears were running down her cheeks. I have never forgotten that moment. It really upset me and still does when I think about it. It underlined how hard it was for all of them to have to move on and start again. In my opinion the Church of England has no consideration for families in ministry. Ordinations (the formal service of becoming a priest) happen before the end of term so following it I had had to return to Nottingham with the children so they could complete the term. Not an ideal beginning and as you have read things were going to get a lot worse!

## FIRST CURACY

The house we had was very pleasant and I was pleased to be near the sea, though Norfolk doesn't compare with Cornwall! It also felt a long way from the rest of the country! I was very aware of the upheaval for the children but the schools we found them were very good and they seemed to settle in quite quickly and happily. I was expecting a baby in the December and was not working, so at least they had the stability of me being there for them all the time and they were very excited when Kimberley was born three days before Christmas! We made some lovely Christian friends in the church, some of whom we are still in contact with. I know many people saw Andy as an answer to their prayers and I remember with great affection one elderly couple who were so thrilled with the injection of life into the church and to be part of our house-group. Humanly I can see now that the vicar must have felt threatened and jealous so when we discovered what we did about him he obviously decided to turn things on their head and use it against us as a reason for Andy to be forced out. Andy has said he doesn't remember why we didn't speak out when we were summoned before the Bishop. We had discussed it and I do remember. It was because he thought it right to follow Jesus' example. Jesus was silent before his accusers when unjustly accused. We have discussed it since and both agree that we should have spoken out the truth of the situation to the Bishop. There were other wrong things not mentioned here. Whether the outcome would have been any different I don't know. We were dismissed with a prayer out of the prayer book!

I do remember with some clarity the drive back from Norwich in the same car as the Vicar. Andy was driving and I was in the back seat, totally distraught, trying to contain my tears. This was the Spring Term of our second year there. Brandon had just moved up to High School and Tammy to Middle School and seemed happy. How could we tell them we had to move again? I wrote to the Bishop asking that we could at least not move until after Spring Harvest which we were going to in the Easter Holidays. Yet again there was absolutely no care for the family by the Church Establishment and we were hounded out like criminals. Well that's how it felt to me. It was a good job that by this stage we had such a strong marriage relationship, the situation caused no conflict between us, if anything it drew us even closer together. I was upset for us but utterly distressed for our children. I could not believe we could be treated like this. Even as I write after all these years I get emotional about the whole episode and do not want to dwell on it. We had been there less than two years.

## MOVING ON

We were 'moved on' into a Team Ministry in Norwich where there were three churches and another curate as well as Andy. We were welcomed by a lovely Vicar and his wife and Andy was given charge of the church on a council estate. I didn't even think of it at the time but the fact he was given this responsibility immediately would seem to suggest that the 'powers that be' knew he wasn't to blame for what had happened previously! Brandon, Barnaby and Tammy had to start new schools in the Summer Term and Brandon and Tammy had only started new High and Middle Schools two terms previously. At least Barney and Tammy were at the same school and they had always got on particularly well. Brandon was not impressed that he had to wear a blazer (!) and I knew he was angry and upset. He refused to go at all for the first few days and I had to force him into the car and take him to the gates. I then went home and cried. It was so unfair. I suppose it was good for me that I had the 'distraction' of having to function to look after Kimberley who was only sixteen months when we moved.

However things are never all bad and we gradually adjusted, helped in some ways by not being too far away from Gorleston so I could maintain some contact with friends. I probably spent quite a bit of time on the phone! Fred and Vera the elderly couple I mentioned earlier had been so upset for us. Fred came and helped paint our lounge and helped Andy re-erect the greenhouse we had bought only twelve months previously. (Most people would not buy such things knowing that you would eventually have to move, but I suppose it illustrates that wherever we have lived we have wanted to make it 'home'.)

For the first few weeks I drove Brandon and Barney back for Sea Scouts but obviously that was not sustainable. Just one of many losses. Bethany was born on February 29th 1988 and brought great joy to us all. All our children have always loved babies and Beth has always thought it unfair that she was the youngest and didn't have a baby brother or sister!

The church gradually grew and flourished, was family orientated and once again we made some good friends. Andy was welcomed and fully involved in the community, including the schools and a GP surgery which held regular multi-disciplinary meetings for professionals to discuss and support families with problems. (Perhaps they should have discussed us!) Lack of money continued to be an issue and I had been doing agency nursing including quite a lot of twilight shifts and nights. Eventually I accepted a permanent part-time post and at last started to pay some superannuation, which I am very pleased about now! I suppose we knew that we wouldn't be able to stay there but I couldn't cope with contemplating another move and there was perhaps an element of ostrich style 'head in the sand'. However, equally, as time went on everyone wanted us to stay, the work was growing and it seemed so right. The other curate was leaving and we knew that if we went the church would be left with no leadership. Apart from that we so didn't want to uproot the children yet again. Barney was already choosing his GCSE options, Tammy was about to join him at High School, Brandon would be leaving with little in way of GCSE success but was committed to his sport and planning to look for a job. Our house was much too small and not on the estate. However, behind the church (that's a grand name for what was a sort of pre-fab building!) there was a reasonable size plot of land. On several occasions we stood there and discussed how a clergy house could be built there and the area would have so benefited by that sort of commitment rather than someone coming in from outside. However, it was not to be. I do not remember the timing of the process or how we told the children we had to move again, but I do remember sobbing on the last day as I hoovered the house. In case you are getting the wrong impression of me I am generally a person in quite good control of my emotions! Yet again I was leaving good friends. One in particular lived only two doors away. She was also a nurse and we saw each other most days as we looked after each other's children when we were working. I had been present at the home delivery (unplanned!) of her little girl a few months after Beth was born and it was a friendship I valued so much. I was already feeling very lonely but again I think it drew Andy and I closer and closer. We had to be each other's best friend because everyone else was transient.

## MOVING ON – AGAIN

I remember the day we moved in 1990 standing in the lounge of the Vicarage which was to be our home for the next nineteen years, though of course we were not to know that at the time. It was actually a five year contract, after which the 'license' had to be renewed, so even now in a Vicar's post there was no long term security. Yet again the Induction Service was before the end of term so Barney and Tammy (14 and 12 now) were staying with friends to complete the term and Brandon was not coming at all. It all seemed so wrong. Kim and Beth were asleep and we just stood in each other's arms feeling overwhelmed by having to face yet another new start. I was so concerned for our three older children and the thought of having to get to know all new people again seemed too much.

The positives for me were the house which, though not big by Vicarage standards, compared to what we had had, was wonderful. The garden was also big and, although nothing had been done to it, it had loads of potential. We had invested in a climbing frame which was to provide loads of fun for many children over the coming years. It was delivered directly to the house and Andy started to erect that before our furniture had arrived! Our years at college and frequent moves had resulted in us re-mortgaging our property and acquiring other loans so I needed to find work quickly. I soon started doing Bank Nursing at the local hospital, as well as some supply teaching, until early the next year when I secured a post as a Staff Nurse on the Twilight District Nursing Service. Kimberley started school in the September and poor Barney and Tammy had to face new schools yet again. Tammy had to do another 'final' year at Middle School (why isn't there standardisation across the country?) and Barney had to change his previously selected GCSE choices as the same subjects were not available. I felt so sorry for them and so helpless. It was only later that I realized how much they protected us from knowing the extent of the hurt and difficulties they went through. Children protecting parents is the wrong way around. I was busy juggling family life, work and trying to support Andy at church which, as he has described, wasn't all plain sailing, so I'm sure I wasn't as aware as I should have been.

I made time to do lots of gardening which has always been therapeutic to me. Andy did loads of heavy work, digging out ponds, planting trees and shrubs and digging out a vegetable plot. The greenhouse came with us and had to be put together bit by bit yet again! It has been productive here for nineteen years and will remain for the new occupants of the Vicarage to use! For a long time the garden looked beautiful with many hanging baskets etc and a summer house that was well used by Kim and Beth and friends for sleepovers as well as a place to escape to for Andy and I! In the last few years we just have not had the time to maintain it like that. It needs some new input! We've had lots of fun times in the garden over the years, especially barbeques for Sunday lunch. We had a large paddling pool and a hose pipe and many church families can reminisce about being soaked in the Vicarage garden! Lots of games were played and of course cricket matches featured too, especially when Brandon came back to live – or maybe they just got more competitive!

When Brandon had his head injury in 1993 he sounded so poorly on the phone and I was really concerned. I just told him I was coming to get him and that was that. I don't think there was ever any discussion about him going back to Norwich. It was a relief to have him home again though obviously not without its difficulties. It couldn't have been easy for Barney to have to share a room again as they are very different characters. Brandon made up for the lost years by not leaving again till he married in 2003!

I was gradually increasing my working hours and did the Community Nursing Degree between 1995 and 1997, alongside my thirty hours a week as a District Nurse. In 1998 I accepted a full time Sister's post in Kidderminster, I was also very involved in church activities so life was very busy. Throughout my years of District Nursing I had been increasingly drawn towards Palliative Care and completed an Open University course in the subject after finishing my degree. I still find it such a privilege to care for the dying and their families, albeit at times exceedingly sad and stressful too. I'm sure my own personal experience of bereavement and its effects on the wider family contributed to my moving into this area of work. In 2000 I became a Community Clinical Nurse Specialist for Marie Curie and in 2004 moved to my current post, which is a joint role between the Community and Macmillan Unit.

Andy has chronicled some of the highs and lows of church life and I have always tried to support him, but don't think I have ever been seen as a traditional vicar's wife (whatever that is!) But then he's not a traditional vicar! Some might say I was type cast in the Pantomimes, I was always the Wicked Witch! Andy said no one else could play it as well, I'm not sure if that was a compliment! Actually I did also play Jane of Tarzan and Jane fame which involved swinging onto the stage on a rope!

A low time occurred for me in 1999 when we finally sold our house in Nottingham ending up with only a few thousand pounds after over twenty five years of paying a mortgage. This was because we had re-mortgaged several times over the years just to keep our heads above water. The future seemed bleak at that point and I really had to struggle to stay positive and trust that God would provide for our needs. Andy tried to encourage me by saying that when others retired they would take their home so much for granted whereas for us it would be exciting because we would so appreciate it. I'm not sure how much comfort that gave me at the time but the words obviously entered my subconscious because I remember it now as it is so true. It was in February, two years later, after a discussion while walking on the cliffs in Yorkshire, good mortgage advice, and a 110% loan from the now infamous Northern Rock (to whom we are very grateful) that we were able to start again. We saw the property on March 8th and got completion on May 1st. We felt it was meant to be! It was wonderful to have a little property in Yorkshire only five minutes from the beach and with sea views! We had some lovely times there and for a while assumed it would eventually be our retirement home. However it was small, had no drive, only a downstairs loo and we made the decision three years later that we needed to relocate back to Worcestershire where all our children still live.

Another low time (understatement!) came for me in 2003 when I was diagnosed with depression. In retrospect I can see it came on gradually but it was a new experience for me and I didn't recognize the warning signs. I like working with doctors but hate having to see them as a patient. I do wonder if this has its roots in my childhood experience of losing my mother. We had a wonderful old fashioned family GP who was very supportive of my father after my mother's death. Even though we lived in the country he would always do home visits if I were poorly. I remember being horrible to him, kicking and screaming and trying to hide under the bed clothes. Perhaps I subconsciously blamed him for my mother's death. Anyway in 2003 I eventually saw my GP and was so grateful for his perception and understanding. One of the worst aspects of my depression was that I seemed to totally lose my faith which, after nearly forty years of being a Christian, was a terrible experience. Fortunately for me my doctor, who has since retired, was not only a Christian but also a non-stipendiary minister so he understood some of the pressure I felt under. Another GP might have considered sectioning me on hearing that one of my worst problems was an inability to believe in God! I kept a journal through this period and the actual time of feeling I believed nothing was in fact only a few weeks but seemed much longer. I eventually recovered completely, through a combination of anti-depressants, time off work and a lot of tender loving care, understanding and support from Andy.

Like many things in life it was not an experience I would have chosen, but I learned through it and hope I became more empathetic to other people. It certainly enabled me to see the warning signs in Andy about a year later. In response to a request from me the same GP came to see Andy at home. It is not easy for a vicar's wife to admit to a diagnosis of depression.

It is much harder when you are the Vicar! Andy had to have some time out and I'm sure probably went back to church too soon, but it was difficult. Afonso was coming over from Portugal and it was almost Christmas. He never really regained his previous energy levels, maybe he would have had he taken longer to complete his recovery. Maybe it was just time to slow down! I'm sure my own experience helped me help him through this period, and through all these things our love has grown.

In the same way as many others I am grateful for Andy's ministry at Christchurch and have learned so much both from his teaching but also just by being with him. It has also been a privilege to be involved with him in so many people's lives during our time here. In recent years life at the Vicarage has become much quieter as gradually all the children have left home and our pets have reduced in number. There used to be seemingly constant comings and goings and there was always someone around to look after things if we were away! The empty nest scenario has finally happened! I can understand why couples who have grown apart find it difficult but we are treasuring this time together.

## LOOKING AHEAD

We are both certain that now is the right time for us to leave Christchurch so that makes thinking about the future easier and there are many aspects of it we are looking forward to. However that does not mean there will not be a real sense of loss, sadness and concerns too. This will have been our family and church home for nineteen years. I usually take Josh and Joseph (our grandsons) to church and they like going to the front to sing with Grandpa. I think they will miss that and hope they remember it in years to come. I'm sorry that our future grandchildren won't have known Grandpa in his 'vicar' role! But hopefully there will be benefits too! It will certainly be strange for us initially not having Sundays 'pre-planned' as it were, although Sunday lunch will continue as a Kelso institution!

We are so grateful for Mulligans. It was the first property we saw in Worcestershire and once again we got completion amazingly quickly. It seemed meant to be! We have a stone in the rockery by the fish pond engraved with Browning's words "Grow old along with me, the best is yet to be". I hope Andy and I have many years ahead to grow old together, but you don't do my job without being aware of the fragility of life and the reality of death. One out of one us will die, that's an indisputable statistic! We know one can take nothing for granted and must appreciate each day as it comes. I do not want to envisage life without Andy, nor would want him to be left alone. A wise Christian taught me many years ago that God does not give us grace to deal with imaginary situations, only the present and I have never forgotten that. As Christians we believe that our times are in His hands (Psalm 31 v 15), that our days were ordained for us before our birth
(Psalm 139 v16). We know too that God has plans to give us a hope and a future (Jeremiah 29 v11-13), both in this life and the one to come. However I have to be honest and say that I am hoping and praying for some good years ahead before we move on to the one to come!

I look forward (with some trepidation!) to new beginnings, new outreach, new friendships, new church (that's quite scary!) and keeping chickens! I also look forward to retaining and building existing friendships on a different basis, and being able to go away for a weekend! I know once we have made the move I shall look back with nostalgia, amongst other things, because that's the way I am! As regards work I am looking forward to reducing my hours in the foreseeable future so it's altogether a time of great change!

# REFLECTIONS

We have retraced some aspects of our lives as a family in the writing of this book and for me it has been quite an emotional process. I have never understood people who say they have no regrets when they look back on their lives. I have lots and these have been highlighted even more as I have read our children's contributions. Most of what they have written I already knew but seeing in black and white, the difficult times they all had through their childhood and young adult years is painful to me. Obviously as a mother I feel guilty for not having been able to protect them better and regret some of the decisions we made which may have made things worse. For example, moving to Nottingham when Andy could have gone to a nearby Theological College, and the school we sent Brandon to in Nottingham, albeit with the best of intentions, and not speaking out in Gorleston. I think we all look back and wonder "What if?"

One of my biggest personal "what ifs" is in relation to my working, which was always driven by financial need not any desire on my part for a career. I would have loved to have been able to be a full time at home wife and mum. Had that been possible I do wonder whether, in spite of all the moves, life might have been that bit easier for the children. I know I just wasn't available enough just to talk and to sense their needs and problems and I will always be sorry for that. So often day to day life was so busy and often seemed to be about surviving! This of course is the scenario for so many young families today, where mothers have no choice about going out to work and children are spending hours watching television and playing computer games. Our society is already reaping the consequences.

It is perhaps ironic that much of my work involves helping support families through difficult and often tragic times. I am grateful to have had a job which is so rewarding and I am told many people have benefited from my input over the years, but.......? What if? When I was doing my nursing degree I had to apologize to Kim and Beth for being bad tempered one evening. I explained that it was the last assignment for the year. Beth said "Will you be normal again then Mum?" She was eight. I have never forgotten that. However like many others I had no choice and at least all our children grew up with an awareness that money doesn't grow on trees! So overall there are many "what ifs," which none of us can ever know the answer to and in one sense regrets are futile because we cannot change the past.

However as long as we don't become morbid it is not a bad thing to reflect on the past because we can learn from it and allow it to shape our present and future positively. Of course to a degree this happens with no effort on our part, for all of our characters are partly formed by past experiences. But I believe we can and should also make a conscious effort to learn from the past on a daily basis. Personally I wish I had prayed more consistently over the years and I cannot use the excuse of not being aware of the importance of this. It's not that I didn't pray but it was a bit hit and miss! Thank goodness for the grace of God! In recent years we have prayed together on a daily basis especially for our children and family as well as day to day issues. It's one of many areas that Andy is more disciplined in than me and I'm so grateful for his positive influence.

When at college we were given a talk by some previous students who had gone on into ministry. The only thing I remember them saying was not to expect or try to make real friends in your parish, you needed to have friends away from where you were ministering. I remember being horrified by this at the time and it was only many years and a lot of hurt later that I realized the wisdom of the words. It was not just losing friendships because of the moves, but also, over the years being let down, by people we really thought were friends. I suppose it is the nature of the role that one is seen as being slightly "different". We must have been in Redditch for almost fifteen years before people finally stopped asking us how much longer we would be here! I don't blame them for that, after all previous incumbents had only ever stayed for five years, but it had the effect of making one feel an outsider, not truly part of the community. These things have probably made me withdraw a bit over the years and certainly made Andy and I value one another as best friends. I do look forward to being Andy and Charm, Mum and Dad, Grandma and Grandpa rather than the vicar and his wife! Having said all of that I know we have also been in a privileged position, we have got to know some wonderful people and have greatly valued the faithful support and prayer we have received.

## FINALLY!

When I read what our children have written I am amazed and grateful that none of them blamed us for what has happened in their lives, not even when it was happening. They all wrote their contributions very quickly, spontaneously and with no collusion! In spite of everything they have all grown into mature, sensible and sensitive adults of whom I am very proud. It is interesting that they all say that the difficult times they experienced helped develop their characters and make them the people they are. It underlines what I said at the beginning about the child being father of the man. In a Christian context Paul says in Romans 5 v 3 that suffering produces perseverance, and perseverance character, and character hope! The principle is there! I believe they all know how much they are loved and valued as individuals and, as I think they have all said, we really enjoy being together as a family. So, we must have done something right! However I also see it as God honouring Andy for his faithfulness to Him and I do believe God's hand of protection has been on our family. Their anger and hurt has been directed at God and the "church". I am sure God enabled that because He knew that for us to handle that as well would be more than we could have borne. My prayer for each of them now as adults is that God will "restore the years the locusts have eaten" (Joel 2 v25). I believe God's Word when Paul says in Romans 8 v28 that "in all things God works for the good of those who love Him, who are called according to His purpose." We are all called, and have to respond as individuals and our adult children are each responsible for "right choices". Hopefully they will be encouraged by their Dad's story! Brandon, Barney, Tammy, Kim and Beth thank you so much for your love over the years and for your part in developing my character!

## REALLY FINALLY!

I'm sure one doesn't normally dedicate individual chapters in books but we've never been ones to bow to convention! I have to dedicate my chapter to Andy!

When I was at such a low ebb in 2003, I remembered my thoughts back in the 1970s when I felt I was doing 'all the giving' in our relationship. I was very aware of how Andy had more than made up for that over the years. I wrote in my journal at the time that although I was struggling with faith in God I was actually having God's love shown to me through Andy on a daily basis. Andy's decision to reveal in this book some of what happened in the early days of our marriage was not easy for either of us Some things one wants to forget and leave behind for ever. The reason we have chosen to mention them is to give hope to others who may be questioning and doubting if their relationship can survive. Our story shows that far more than survival is possible!

In Ephesians 5 v 25 Christian men are told to love their wives as Christ loved the church. That love was totally sacrificial. It is in that context that Christian wives are told to 'submit to their husbands in everything' (Ephesians 5 v 24). Of course that causes a great outcry from the feminist lobby, even within Christian circles. But I can tell you from first hand experience there is no problem when you have a husband who is endeavouring to love you with a love which puts you first. I'm not talking super-spiritual things here, but practicalities, tea in bed, shopping, washing, all sorts of things. I have seen in Andy how the love and power of God can be outworked in a person's life. It is usually a lifelong process. Andy has always said that God's way is marinating not microwaving!

We are both the same people we were when we first met. That inner core which I mentioned at the beginning which makes 'us', 'us', is still there. Andy is still the same person I fell in love with over forty years ago, - and yet we are different! Years and experience change us all. Some people may become embittered, cynical or simply resigned by what life throws at them. On the other hand I'm sure we all know some who never seem to have any problems and are blessed with money, health, and an optimistic outlook and it doesn't seem fair! But we all know 'life' isn't fair. As Christians we have the privilege of having the Holy Spirit within us to direct and challenge and use the effect of years and experience. We have to daily make a choice to allow that. Andy has chosen to do that over the years and I am learning alongside him!

We have both had difficulty when reading so many Christian books which seem in many ways unrelated to the real world and have that 'happy ever after atmosphere' which has left us feeling "Well it's alright for them but..." I hope this book doesn't evoke that response, but I have to end on a positive note! You may remember at the beginning of this chapter I mentioned my teenage certainty that I would meet someone and know he was the right one for me. Well I did and he was and still is! It just shows teenage dreams can come true! I am so grateful to Andy for so much. Of course love changes over the years from the heady thing it is when you are young, but the amazing thing is, which you can't believe when you are young and in love, it actually gets better and deeper and all sorts of things! We love being together, doing things together, having fun! We miss each other when we are apart and almost always speak on the phone during a working day. The really good thing is, unlike years ago, we rarely argue now! I feel honoured, privileged and grateful to be his wife.

Thank you Andy, for everything.

## Chapter Seven:

## OUR CHILDREN'S CHAPTER

**BRANDON WRITES**:

Early Days    I remember Watford back in the 1970s! I had a milk truck and used to make regular deliveries to the kitchen! We lived in a terraced house, which I think was deceptively bigger than it looked. I remember Mum working evenings at the RAC and hearing Dad come home from work on his scooter.

However my most vivid memories are of sunny Sunday afternoons in Cassiobury Park. I had a shiny new cricket ball in my hand and on my long run up I'd think I was Ian Botham, and the batsman (dad) was Boycott. For me it was a real contest, not just a game! I really wanted to get that wicket! It may have taken ages and Dad may have just let me, but in my selective memory I can still see the middle stump cart wheeling out of the ground! Like I said, it wasn't about a gentle game with a tennis ball being slogged only onto the leg side. I was taught to be competitive, to select my shots and to have the will to win. In the winter the sport was rugby with lots of tackling and scoring tries, so Dad nurtured my sporting ability from an early age. In later years it has made me still want to be a winner and not give up, not just in sport but in life. It took me much longer to learn to accept defeat gracefully but I think I have just about got there now!

We never had much money but Mum and Dad always made sure Christmas was special, well, it is, it is Jesus' birthday! Father Christmas was real (still is) and it always seemed so magical. Opening our presents was great and confirmed that Father Christmas was real, Mum and Dad could never have afforded all that! In 1979 I got my first Tottenham shirt! Wow! Christmas at Mum and Dad's is still special to this day.

I remember Scalectrix. It probably drove Mum mad but Dad, Barney and I would spend hours (and Dad too much money) playing with it. Of course I was very competitive, which would cost me as my car would come flying off the track! I could go on and on; as I write memories come flooding back, - I remember some of Dad's school productions, particularly Joseph and the Dramathon. These were my best days with Dad, and although it's not nice to say, when Dad got called into the Church things were different. It wasn't Dad's fault but looking back, things changed a lot and I admit I hated God for this and carried this feeling with me for many years. If I'm honest I still look back and think maybe things would have been different if it wasn't for the 'Church'.

**NOTTINGHAM:** I did have some good times in Nottingham. Dad took me to Notts Forest and County Football matches and I joined my first football team, Bramcote Cubs under 11s! We had a really good park near our house and I remember sledging there with Dad. But what I really remember is my new school, even now the thought of it makes me shiver. To be fair, at the time I'm sure Mum and Dad didn't know how much I hated it. To me it was a horrible place. I had to wear a cap, shorts and say the Lord's Prayer aloud everyday! Since I thought God had taken me to the school I wasn't pleased! Inside I think I was really upset, why did we have to move at all? I knew the answer was that Dad had been called by God. Boy, I really hated God!

Still, I must say we still had some great family times, particularly holidays and Christmas but I was feeling that God took all of Dad's time. I knew Dad and Mum were training for new careers but I wanted to go back to Watford and have my Dad back. My perception was that the church was ruining my life.

**NORFOLK:** From Nottingham we moved near to Great Yarmouth. When I thought things couldn't get any worse, they did! Although I had to cope with another new school and the final year of Middle School, it was a lot better than the last hell hole and I had an old fashioned type of teacher who I respected and really worked for. The church where Dad was a curate had about as much life in it as a flat pint of real ale! It was horrible, and you know what? I blamed God! However my football continued to improve. I played for the school and soon got signed up for a local Under 12s and 13s. I don't remember that Dad could come to many games – I knew I was good and wanted to show my Dad. But he had his work cut out at the church and boy did he! He was turning it from a morgue into somewhere with some life. People responded to him and I could tell he was great at the job and a little part of me could see why God had wanted him. But just as I was starting to enjoy life again, bang! This time we were being forced to move. I didn't know all the details but this sealed it for me, God was really, really gone for me. I just couldn't understand it. He wanted my Dad; Dad did a great job and then was kicked out. Why?

**HELLESDON:** If I say I finally felt this was home, yet also say it was where I hit rock bottom it may seem like a contradiction. We continued to have good family times, including going to Spring Harvest, which I loved, as well as holidays in Yorkshire and Cornwall. I always loved Cornwall and could never understand why we couldn't just move there!

I had to start a new High School in the Summer Term, having just done two terms at another one. Not easy for any one. But when you are a Vicar's son everyone knows and it doesn't win you friends! Well I was going to show them what a 'Bible Basher' could do! I don't think Mum and Dad knew the half of it, until now. I hated everything to do with church, although just how much I think I hid quite well. I played football on Sunday mornings and wasn't forced to go to church. After a week or so at school I was sick of the constant jibes and jokes. I had so much anger that had built up in me. One break time I punched the culprit on the nose and by lunchtime had fought with the so called toughest boy in our year. I still had that will to win! We had a rematch the next day and I beat him up again. I was gaining respect and I liked this! As it turned out, after my Dad had done a few assemblies he was nicknamed the 'cool vic' because he wore normal clothes and Nike trainers! I had no more mickey taking, I was now one of the 'in' crowd. I didn't need God, I had my mates! We had a big gang and used to hang around the park and shops smoking, drinking and generally getting into trouble. Now I was older I could express my anger with God by being a total rebel. Some of the things I got up to were terrible. Imagine how my Dad must have felt when the police turned up on the doorstep! I would play truant from school and forge my Mum's signature on sick notes and did no work at school. I was cool in the eyes of my so called 'mates' and that was all that mattered to me at the time.

Yet again I was aware that my Dad was doing a fantastic job at the church. Luckily for me my sport was still very important to me and I would go as far as saying that it was probably sport that prevented me from drifting into a really bad life at this time. I have found out over the years that three of our gang have died from drug overdoses and at least four have been in and out of prison and are very likely still taking drugs.

I was now playing a high standard of football with what would now be the equivalent of Norwich City Youth Academy. I played cricket for the school and also joined a local cricket club, and this was thanks to those early days with my Dad. I also enjoyed having 'little sisters', they were a positive in these difficult years.

Mum and dad have always had animals and we loved them but another great sadness in Norwich was when our border collie, Eppy, died. I lay with her on the kitchen floor and was heartbroken because she had grown up with us and was one of the family. It was another great loss.

With all the doom and gloom, and although God and me were by no means straight, I found myself playing in the Church Football Team! My Dad had decided to enter a local Christian league competition! The first year was awful and we didn't win a game! However, the second year we won the cup and I saw my Dad achieve this by giving the team belief and desire (and making them get fit!) I could see my Dad how I wanted to, I just wished we hadn't missed those other years. The team continued to do well under Dad's captaincy. However after just three years and with the church growing and wanting him to stay, he couldn't because he was 'only' a curate, my parents had to move on again. I knew they didn't want to either but they had no choice. But this time I wasn't going! I was three months short of my 18th birthday when Mum, Dad, Barney, Tammy Kim and Beth moved to Redditch.

A Christian couple had offered me accommodation and I had found a job, so my parents agreed I could stay. I was committed to a good football and cricket team and had been offered a trial for Norwich City. On the downside I was still drinking and involved with a bad crowd. They understood how important the sport was to me and how difficult the previous moves had been and I suppose felt guilty.

Looking back, maybe I should have gone with them; I could always have played a high standard of sport in Redditch. But I thought that if I went God would win again so I would not go, I would not move home again! The trouble was, after they went it never was home any more and I spent many evenings alone feeling so unhappy. It didn't help that I was sharing a room with a really 'messed up' person who has since died of a drug and alcohol related illness. Many times I wanted to call Dad and go home, but I didn't speak to him much. There would be phone calls to Mum in the evenings when Dad was often out. I missed my Dad so much but I wouldn't budge because if I did God would win! After all, he got my Dad! These days are at the back of my memory now and I don't think I have ever really spoken about how things really were. But I was falling and fast. I was still doing my sport but the Norwich thing fell through, whether due to my ability or life-style I will never know. I was staggering home from nightclubs, gambling places, experimenting with drugs and fighting. I ended up in a police cell on more than one occasion. How I never got a criminal record I don't know. The couple I was living with had no idea what was going on and were easy to deceive with lies. I even stole a digger once and drove it home when drunk, a distance of about four miles. Inside I felt awful and couldn't see a way out. I was losing my old 'friends', they no longer seemed 'cool'. I even started to hate them. Luckily the cricket club gave me some good company and for that last summer in Hellesdon I felt ok.

Then one Sunday morning in February 1993 I sustained a serious head injury and was in hospital for four days. I had gone to the match following an all night drinking session. My parents were on holiday in Yorkshire that week. When they got home the next Saturday Mum got out of Dad's car and straight into hers and drove to Norwich to fetch me. One way or another God got me home! Maybe I started to like Him again from that point! Back home again and this time there were to be no more moves until I finally 'flew the nest' for good which took quite a few years.

When I look back I know God decided Dad's path and he had to take it. Dad has done so much good work, helped hundreds of people find the truth, a purpose in life, and love and peace. This is the big picture and more important than anything I can moan about, although I still wonder what life would have been like if we hadn't had to move at all. I admit I still have a battle of my own to fight but my Mum and Dad always gave me their love. It's easier to speak to Mum about things, I just don't do it much but that probably goes for a lot of us. I love my Dad. He has given his life to battle against Satan and all that goes with running a church, and I'm sure he will still do more. But Dad has earned his retirement and I hope he and Mum have many happy years in their new home.

I would just like to add a postscript! Taking away the moves and church, in case this all seems too awful, as a family we also had some great times together and I do have some good memories! Holidays, Christmas, family celebrations, growing up with Barney and Tammy and then the arrival of Kim and Beth were all great. It really wasn't all bad stuff, it was just the moving I found so hard, as I know we all did. However we have come through strongly as a family and now it is growing bigger! I am married to my wonderful wife Penny, who I wouldn't have met if I hadn't come to Redditch! We have two smashing sons, Joshua and Joseph, and are now expecting twins! The battle goes on and we all need to try to help Dad more because he is only retiring from running a church! God needs more disciples like my Dad, and who knows, another Kelso may be chosen to follow Dad's path.

Mum and Dad, Grandma, Grandpa, thanks for everything you have done. Love, Brandon and Penny.

**BARNEY WRITES**:

My Dad has asked me to write a few words about my childhood memories as he is putting a book together, which you are probably reading now! Where can I begin! My earliest memory is living in Watford, who I still support with a passion! I will tell you why I think this is, later.....I remember walking to school, playing on my bike with friends in the road we lived in (which was Bradshaw Road I think!) and without asking anyone number 52 rings a bell! I might be completely wrong! I also remember being a mouse in a stage production. Funny what stays in your head! I also remember the day we were told we were moving to Nottingham. As a child of seven, I think, I didn't want to move but there is not a lot you can do at that age is there!

I remember Nottingham well and settled in fairly quickly, again we had a good life. I do recall not liking it as much as Watford. I missed going to drama classes. Dad was training to be a vicar and mum was training to be a nurse! Sadly before we knew it we were told we were moving again to a place called Gorleston-On- Sea. Dad had finished his training and had been offered a job there. I remember asking why? Why did we have to move again and it was because of work obviously, which I understand now but as a child it is so much more difficult.

Gorleston was a great place! One of the main reasons was because we could walk to the sea from our house! Wow! We lived on a main road opposite a park, with a hospital behind our house. So we had lots to do as children and we had an open fire in the house (that might be why I like them so much now, and wish I had one!). I settled in very quickly and made some good friends at school. I had my first girlfriend there! She was called Donna Boggis! I also made a really good friend called Justin whose family went to the local church. I was also a choir boy there!! What…..did I just write that!! All I can remember of Gorleston are good memories. Oh yes and Brandon and I were Sea Scouts! Much better than being a normal scout I tell you!!! Oh, and we had another sister, Kimberley! The only sad memory I have of Gorleston was the day we were told by Mum and Dad we were moving to Norwich. I assumed Dad had finished his two year stint of being a curate and he was now a fully fledged vicar! I was proud of my dad for being a vicar, but being told we were moving again was hard and still brings back sad thoughts. It became more difficult with age. I know Brandon took it really hard. Mum and Dad obviously protected me well, I had no idea at the time of the real reason for the move. It's strange, as I write more memories of those days come flooding back.

Norwich was only an hour or so away from Gorleston but it seemed like millions of miles away when we first arrived. I think this was the first time children at school made fun of my name and made more fun when they found out my Dad was a vicar. I don't understand why children are so cruel. To me, my Dad was my dad not a vicar! This only lasted a week or so. When they found out I was fairly good at most sports I was soon accepted. I made some truly great friends at Norwich. Ian was my best friend. When we first moved I was in the last year of middle school. The following year I moved up to the local High School. Brandon had become very popular although I remember him having a few problems to start with! We had another sister arrive in Norwich, Bethany! I loved Norwich, mum and dad worked very hard and I remember looking after my sisters quite a lot! Strangely this is the first time I really remember going to church! Dad arrived at a church with a very small congregation and he left with a very large congregation! It showed he did a good job and should have been allowed to stay! I have two sad memories of

Norwich; Eppy, our dog who I had known since my first ever memory, died of old age. I remember being heart broken. The second sad memory was the day we were told we were moving. This was the hardest of all the moves. It makes me feel sad now! It caused a lot of heartache and arguments. I was truly hurt and as I was older found it very hard to take. I loved school and Norwich and I had made some great friends who I believe would still be great friends to this day if we had not moved. I also had been going out with a girl called Rebecca Rose for around a year. I remember the day I had to go, walking to see her at the end of her road we both cried and kissed each other goodbye..... It was also very hard leaving my best friend Ian. I not only got on so well with him, but his mum and dad as well. I still miss him in many ways. This is where Brandon stayed; he was 17 and didn't want to move. I wanted to stay as well.....

Redditch was the worst place we lived I think..... I hated it from day one. It got a little better over time you will be pleased to hear! Moving at nearly 15 is not good. I know both myself and Tammy had a hard time for a few months. We had a lot of people at school being horrible about dad being a vicar, stupid comments, but hurtful in many ways. My Dad is my dad, as I have previously said, and I am very proud of what he has done in his life. He is without doubt an amazing person! When people make comments about your Dad it hurts. Looking back it was one of the lowest points in my life. I managed to make a few friends again, mainly because I was OK at sport and when kids find out you are not a 'geek' you are accepted, sad really! I do remember hearing Tammy cry herself to sleep a few times in those first few weeks and for some reason I did not go and see if she was OK. We were quite close and this move made us even more so. Brandon and I had our differences in Norwich but I also missed my big brother. I think me and Tammy were trying to cope in our own private way. I did cry a few times myself and people who know me well know I don't cry about anything really! (It's made me a little emotional for the first time now in writing this!) I think it just shows how much I missed Norwich and my friends and my brother. School was a difficult two years. I made friends but not friends like I had in Norwich. Put it like this, I don't keep in contact with anyone from school and have not seen anyone from that school in many years. Strangely I am now a member of 'Facebook' and many old friends from Norwich have made contact, but none from Redditch! I think that says something in itself!!

This was the first time I really went to church and started to really believe as a Christian. Looking back, this is a good thing! Church, my family and God got me through those lonely years at school and they were lonely at times. I almost couldn't be bothered to make friends. I think I certainly changed as a person. I grew up a lot more quickly and became more sensible! I met a great girl called Sam when I was 15 and I think we helped each other. I'm very grateful for her support and probably have never told her that. Redditch and church life brought me back into the realm of acting! Dad wrote and produced several pantomimes/musicals! I loved them, being involved in all the rehearsals and the actual performances. It brought many people together from the surrounding community and was a massive success! It brings a big smile to my face looking back on them. In many ways I wish I was involved in acting in some way. I loved being on the stage! But boy it is hard work! I often think if I win the lottery I will get one of Dad's shows on in the West End!!

Looking back over all the moves I think we remained close as a family, which helped in a big way. In many ways we were very lucky compared to other people. In the job I do now I see some terrible sights and many broken families and it puts a lot into perspective.  We shared many great holidays together over the years.  I see myself as very lucky that Dad is a Yorkshire man and Mum is a Cornish lady!  We spent some great holidays in both locations.  It also gave me some stability in terms of that's where they were born and bred and I sort of count myself as half Yorkshire and half Cornish!  (If that makes sense!).  I have many fond memories of family holidays and these will always remain in my thoughts.  It's odd when you reach the age of 16/17 that you no longer want to go away with your Mum and Dad.  Now I'm a fully grown man I love going on holiday with them again!

From school I went to college then eventually onto University.  Moving house and around the country has made me become the person I am today (which I think is not a bad person!).  The first three moves were ok, but the last move without a doubt was the hardest.  This is because I think you reach a certain age where it becomes very difficult.  I understand why we had to move but as a child it is so much harder to take in.  I do not blame my parents in any way.  They have been nothing but a support throughout my life and I love them and every member of my family very much.  Although I do not tell them enough, hopefully they all know this.  I feel very lucky to have such a wonderful and loving family.  God remains the most important thing in my life.  I am a Christian and very much enjoyed going to church throughout my childhood.  In many ways going to church helped me through the moves and it gave me an extended family.  Although I have not been to church for quite a few years now I have a little chat with the big man on a daily basis!  It is one of many things I say I need to do, go back to church that is!

Still to this day I am sometimes jealous of people who have lived somewhere all their life.  Why?  Because they can truly call that place home.  I sometimes struggle to say where my home is.  I think this is why I still support Watford with so much passion!  Maybe as I was born there psychologically this is home.  But, as they say, 'Home is where the Heart is' so my home is now where Amanda (my wife) is and where my family lives.

**TAMMY WRITES**:

My earliest memories as a child must have been when I was about 4 or 5 living in Watford in our house with my mum and dad and brothers.  Although my memories are quite vague from this time, I do remember them being happy times.  When we moved to Nottingham I don't really remember having any feelings about this other than it being something new and a bit of an adventure, as I suppose a five year old would.  Looking back and observing children in my adulthood it is amazing how children are so accepting of change and just accept things for what they are, well, up to a certain age anyway, which I'll come to later.

We lived in Nottingham for two or three years I think whilst Dad trained to be a vicar.  Although at the time I don't think it really registered with me what he was doing, he was just my dad first and foremost and the particulars didn't really come into it as a five/six year old.  Now I know.  This was the time my mum was training to be a nurse but again, I think if you asked me back then I probably didn't know this.  All I know is that I missed my mum a lot when she wasn't there as she had to work a lot of night shifts so wasn't there to say goodnight (I don't know how much she was away, it may have been very little, but back then it felt an awful lot).  I remember being very happy at my school here and had a lot of friends.  Our time there was soon to be over and we moved on to Gorleston in East Anglia.

Gorleston again was a nice place to live. We settled in well at the schools. I remember the church we went to there was quite boring and on reflection, now know why, as in comparison to other churches it was much more formal and traditional. Still, it had its advantages! My brother and I joined the choir as you got £1.00 for every wedding that you did, which back then seemed a lot of money! As an adult I now know the troubles that went on at this church, and although as a child at that time I certainly wasn't aware of this. On reflection, although our parents protected us well, we knew something wasn't right. It's amazing how perceptive children are! In Gorleston my little sister Kimberley arrived which was great fun. I know my mum carries a certain amount of guilt thinking that I was no longer the youngest and in some way this affected me. I can honestly say I never felt pushed out with either of my sisters (Bethany came two years later) so I don't know why my mum thinks this!

From Gorleston, we moved on to Hellesdon in Norwich when I was about nine. This was the first time out of all the moves we had to date that I remember feeling different. However I soon made friends here and settled in to school really well. We had an old lady (she seemed old at the time!) who Barney and I used to call our grandma who did the kind of things that you would want a grandma to do. We didn't have our grandparents close by, in fact at this stage I had not even met my dad's mum from what I can recall. I think we saw our friends with their grandparents and we wanted that special relationship too. So this move was more difficult, although once we had moved and started school I soon settled in quickly. The three years we spent here were my fondest memories. Again I had a large circle of friends and more importantly had a best friend, Angela. Along with her and other friends I had a great time both in and outside of school.

The three years here seemed to pass very quickly. It was a real shock when my mum and dad told us we had to move again. I remember thinking how am I going to tell Angela? I plucked up the courage a few days later and told her in the loos at school! We both had a good cry. Mum and Dad had to move with my sisters before the end of the summer term. Barney and I stayed on and I lived with friends from church so we could finish the school term. I remember having a lot of mixed feelings. Although I missed my mum and dad a great deal I remember feeling guilty because when it was time to leave I just didn't want to go. I wanted to stay with all my friends in the happy life that we had created here.

Before we moved to Redditch I remember mum and dad taking us there for the day to visit some schools and see the house we were moving to. The house, the schools, the people we met I hated it all! I just didn't want to move and felt like screaming. Imagine being a twelve year old, having a happy family life, great friends, about to move up to high school with all your friends, basically being completely content with life, to be told you've got to move, and all of this is to be taken away. You have no choice, no one consults with you; you are just a kid. I remember feeling a lot of anger, not at mum and dad but the church. Why have we got to move? Why can't we just stay here?

Still it was not to be and, like it or not, we moved to Redditch. We moved at the beginning of the summer holidays so had no friends, as school didn't start until September. Luckily for me the church had a camping trip planned, which I went along to and it was here I met Catherine. Over the next few years Catherine and I became best friends and were inseparable, although she didn't go to the same school as me so I still had this to contend with. I started school in the September and, because they ran a different schooling system in Worcestershire, had to go in to the last year of middle school again, which was really demoralising as if we'd stayed in Hellesdon I would have been going to High School. This school year was the worst in my whole schooling life. Everyone already had their set group of friends, up until now I had always made friends really easily without thinking about it, but here it was really difficult. It was here I first encountered being made fun of because my dad was a vicar. This was alien to me; I'd never had to deal with this before. At first I just got defensive and had a go back but this seemed to make it worse.

In hindsight I realize this was because they were getting a reaction, which was what they were looking for. So in the end I just ignored them, which did help, but I learned to live with the fact that my Dad's job was a source of amusement for some of the kids and so the jibes were always there. At this time I hated Redditch, I hated everything there and just longed to return to Hellesdon. The only person I could talk to was my brother Barney and Angela, so I used to write her letters. Her letters back were a great source of comfort but at the same time painful, as she used to update me on what all of our friends were up to. It felt that their lives were moving on without me and I was stuck in limbo. I didn't want to live here and I hated the church for making us move here. It was at this time I began to lose weight. I don't really know what started it, whether it was just because I was so unhappy and losing weight meant I was in control. I became obsessed and weighed myself every day. I stopped eating breakfast, threw my lunch away, and did what I could to avoid eating an evening meal. I got down to 7st 1lb, which at 5ft 7 was quite light! I think the turning point was when I moved up to high school and got involved in all the sports, which I excelled in and I suppose my focus changed. So luckily my weight problem took a back seat which I'm very grateful for because looking back I know I was very close to it ending very differently. At this school I had a friend who was anorexic, and was sectioned. I remember going to see her in the unit. It was an awful place, and I thought I never want to end up somewhere like this. Things gradually got better, I made some good friends and life seemed a lot brighter; although I still yearned for my life in Hellesdon, I knew I just had to get on with it. I never felt I could talk to my parents at this time because I knew they were struggling too. Like me I knew that they didn't want to move either and knew they had no choice, so didn't want to burden them with my problems as I knew that this would make them feel guilty but it wasn't their fault.

On reflection of my childhood I am very grateful to my parents. I grew up knowing that, no matter what, I always had their love and support, and something sadly a lot of children grow up without. We didn't have much money but this didn't matter. I have got fantastic memories of all our holidays together camping, doing simple things and I couldn't have wished for more. My advice would be, if you do have a choice, don't move with children passed the age of ten, as from my experience you're setting them up for a turbulent time. I still wonder what my life would have been like if we had stayed in Hellesdon. However my life wouldn't be what it is now if we hadn't moved. Whilst there were some tough times, my childhood and my parents have made me the person I am today. If we hadn't moved to Redditch then I wouldn't have met Brad and we wouldn't be getting married later this year! When things happen in life that you don't want, it is hard to see the positives when all that is evident are the negatives. Well meeting the person I will share the rest of my life with has got to be the biggest positive of them all, and that wouldn't have happened if we hadn't moved to Redditch! I will always be eternally grateful to my mum and dad for being the best parents any child could hope for, and being able to extend that relationship into adulthood, I know how lucky I am to have that.

**KIM WRITES:**

Growing up as a child was different for me compared with Brandon, Barney and Tammy as I only had one move. This was from Norwich to Redditch, and didn't really affect me as I was only four at the time. I remember the day we moved into the Vicarage quite vividly, it was chaos! Marilyn (from the church) came round and collected Beth and myself and we played with her daughter's dolls house and back then I thought it was amazing!

Growing up as a child, well, what can I say? It had its good and bad points, like every child growing up I guess. For me it was slightly different, as being accepted as a Vicar's daughter wasn't easy. Through first school it didn't pose a problem as no one really had opinions, I suppose because we were so young! Going to Middle school was different though, and from the age of eleven until I was fourteen I was bullied just because of Dad's job. I was called names (Bible Basher), spat at, left out of groups, picked on etc.

I found this really difficult to cope with. I couldn't understand why people were so horrible just because Dad was a vicar, especially as they had all loved the assemblies he did when we were younger. Why did his title of vicar make me so different to everyone else? I used to walk home crying, and for a while I couldn't tell Mum and Dad what was going on because I was so embarrassed! Eventually I told them and got moved into the next class. This made my life so much better for a while!

Going to high school was even harder. More people, more groups, more opinions! Dad used to go into schools and do assemblies. I hated it. I was embarrassed but would ask myself, why am I embarrassed? Because of peoples' opinions? or because I was scared of facing being bullied again? I didn't know then and to this day I still don't know the answer. What I do know is that all those opinions and horrible remarks contributed to making me the person I am today. So many people get bullied for many reasons. I know I'm not the only one and probably everyone reading this has had a time in their life where people have judged them for different reasons. I came out of it a much stronger person and will not let it happen to me again. I am not embarrassed by my Dad. I love him and am really proud to be his daughter.

Growing up wasn't all about God and going to church although through church I did meet a lot of people, one of whom really did affect my life. At first I thought she was great and could change so many lives through her experiences with God. After a while I discovered that this person herself was deceived and not the 'woman of God' she claimed to be. She didn't just hurt my family but a lot of other people too and it cost me a good relationship. Even though hate is a strong word at the time I hated her, and even now I look back and feel quite bitter about the way in which she affected not only my family but the church as well. I gave up my bedroom for this person every time she came over to the UK. For a long time after Mum and Dad parted company with her I thought that my room was under some sort of spell. I never really discussed it with Mum and Dad and probably should have. Until then I was committed as a Christian but she caused me to abandon my faith and my life took another direction. Deep down I suppose I know that there is a battle going on and that I cannot forever blame her for my choices.

I've grown up in a loving family for which I'm grateful and always got on with my brothers and sisters, (even though like any family we would have our arguments!) We had great family holidays even though Mum and Dad couldn't really afford them. Even though I went through some tough times I am just a normal person living a normal life just like everyone else. What did I learn from my past? Well, amongst other things I learned that no matter what anyone says or does to try and stop you from doing things in your life that you believe in, you need to persevere because you will come out stronger at the end just like me!

**BETH WRITES**:

When I was asked to write this, I honestly didn't know where to start. I don't have an amazing story to tell, or an awe inspiring testimony to give, but I hope that I can give you a little insight into the realities of growing up in ministry.

Until recently I thought that I'd never been really been affected by dad's ministry, but as the time draws nearer to moving on, I can now see that it has probably had an affect on almost every aspect of my life.

At school, I guess I experienced some mild bullying in the form of name calling, and I have most definitely been called a 'Bible basher' on more than one occasion! I can laugh at this now, but at the time, however much I tried to hide it, it hurt. I hated that some people saw me as different. I hated it more because when they were insulting me, they were also insulting my dad. I remember dad telling me once that when people said anything to me about his job, it wasn't aimed at me, it was aimed at him. This made me angrier, how dare people insult my dad! In a silly way I wanted to protect him, so often I wouldn't say anything when somebody had upset me. I didn't want him to know that I was getting problems at school because of him.

I remember the time when dad first met Pastor Afonso, and I noticed a change in the church and the direction it was going in. The only way I can describe it was I felt things were really becoming 'serious'. I was about 11 and this scared me. I guess it wasn't long after this when my parents, my sister and I went to stay with Afonso and Elizabeth in Portugal. We had a great week and a great time together. I remember taking bags full of sweets and chocolate to share with their children Danny and Sammy. We all laugh at this now. I think we thought that they couldn't get sweets in Portugal! I think this week was good for all of us. I'd met many Pastors and many had come to stay in our home. The relationship that Dad had with Pastor Afonso and Elizabeth felt different, and this helped me to feel relaxed and understand, as best I could at that age, the changes that were happening in the church.

Not long after this time dad came into contact with a preacher from America, and she began staying with us when she came to England. Though I found her quite overwhelming, I saw that my parents really liked her, and I really liked her too. I guess she was in contact with dad and the church for about 3 years and I saw that she had a really good relationship with my parents. I now know that my parents protected me from a lot of what happened in the situation that followed that. However I still noticed things and knew that something wasn't right. I think I was particularly aware of her affect on my sister and seeing my sister upset really upset me too. Pastor Afonso and Elizabeth really supported my parents at this time, and though I was still only quite young, it made me feel so much better knowing the support that Dad had from them, and from others in the church.

Like most teenagers, I just wanted to fit in, and as I got to high school I felt I never really did, no matter how hard I tried. Everything was a big effort, because I was trying extra hard to try and shake off my life long label of 'the vicar's daughter'. I had a large friendship group at school, but no really close friends who I could talk to and often things just felt like a big pretense.

At the age of about 15, I hit a rebellious streak. This side of my personality I definitely take from my dad! Up until this point I'd gone to church regularly and enjoyed it. I'd made a commitment, and knew the truth. However when I joined sixth form the combination of a new part time job with a new found fondness for parties meant I soon stopped and began enjoying lazy Sunday mornings at home. My parents would come home from church and tell me a little about what had happened, telling me that people had asked after me, and I was interested and would like to hear. After a while I got used to not going and quite frequently heard the phrase 'we missed you this morning'! I started to hate hearing about church because I dreaded being told about something that I no longer felt a part of.

Sadly, at this time there weren't many young people in the church. I had no close Christian friends and so at times I felt really alone. I could of course have spoken to my parents but at 16 there are just some things you don't want to talk to your parents about!

For a long time I kept my feelings to myself, and I guess this is what fuelled the next year or so of slipping further away from church and from my faith.

I think I'd become quite distant at home. I could be moody and irritable and I know at times I was really quite difficult to live with. I knew that I was hurting my parents with the way I was acting, but I didn't know how to stop. Though I was trying my hardest to shake off the 'vicar's daughter' image, at this time more than ever I felt a real pressure to be a certain person and I was sick of it. There were times when I really wanted to go to church. I didn't tell mum and dad this. I didn't go because I didn't want people asking me questions about where I'd been.

Throughout my growing up years my parents were amazing. They never put pressure on me to go to church or to do anything I didn't want to do, something people at school couldn't get their heads round. I think their gentle understanding and patience regarding this made a real difference to my attitude towards church.

Every time dad got hurt through someone or something relating to his ministry I became really angry with the church, with dad's job and with God. I remember crying myself to sleep once when I was about 11 saying to God 'Why couldn't my dad just have been normal?' I prayed that God would make him an office worker, a doctor, a builder or something! Somehow I don't think my dad will ever fit into the category of 'normal'!

I've always been so proud of all that my dad was and all that he stood for. I saw the real love that he had for others and the desire that he had to share the truth about Jesus with them. I saw him when he came home on Sundays, exhausted after speaking the truth that morning. I saw him spending hours arranging things for the church, so it hurt and angered me so much when I saw him get hurt or accused by what I saw as the very people he was trying to help.

I'm so grateful to God for blessing me with such wonderful parents. Looking at the difficult childhood that my dad experienced, the love that he is able to show me everyday in his words and his actions amazes me and humbles me so much. It's only now that I know the tough times he had in the past and yet quite honestly I wasn't aware of half of them. I know this demonstrates the remarkable nature of both of my parents. I see the amazing and unconditional love of Jesus demonstrated in every aspect of dad's ministry. I see the passion and fire within him when he preaches, and it is for this reason that I too have a passion for people. The love and security that my parents have given me and the freedom that they gave me to grow and to be me has enabled me to go and love others in this way.

Though it's true that there were times when growing up in ministry were really tough, and times when I longed to just have a 'normal family'. I'm so very grateful for the family that I have and the experiences that we've been through together. Dad's job often meant that he was very busy doing things for the church and there were, and still are, times when I longed for dad just to be my dad. When your dad is a vicar you have to learn to share him with the whole congregation! Despite this my parents have always been there for me, have been ever loving and ever encouraging. I know that I'm so very blessed in this way. There are so many children that just don't get to have this relationship with their parents.

We've had great family times together when it has just been us, and dad has just been Dad. I know that he didn't find it easy to switch off from church on holidays, but he eventually did and I have some lovely memories of family holidays together. My favourite holidays were the times we went to Yorkshire. We always went in wintertime, either February or October so it was always freezing! I remember Dad, Kim and I waking up super early to go and get sweets and a newspaper from the shop every morning before mum had even woken up. Even on holiday dad was always an early riser. We used to go on what seemed like extremely long walks with our numerous dogs too. I'm not so sure I was always thrilled at being dragged across the Yorkshire moors, but it always turned out to be fun! Two occasions I remember specifically. One was trying to learn my 8 times table with dad, the other was singing the songs that Dad had written for the pantomimes at the top of our voices. I can remember dad writing these songs on holiday in Yorkshire. I was once the lucky one and got to hear the preview of a few of the songs he'd written for Treasure Island. Though I think he got me on board to help him out with the actions, either way I felt very privileged! Walking our dogs is something dad and I still like to do together and is still a special time for me. It's a nice time when we can just talk, and often laugh! Recently we went walking and Dad told me he'd found the 'ideal swinging branch'. Although the tree looked to me like it was very much dead he was convinced it was a good idea so lifted me up to have a go. Needless to say the tree was dead and so the large branch came thumping down, just missing our heads...he found this quite amusing!

We also had great family holidays in France. For some unknown reason it was always our tent that got flooded in the thunderstorms, and I have funny memories of the whole family, and incidentally the whole row of fellow campers, desperately trying to remove the flood water with pots, pans and other random kitchen utensils! My dad was always great fun to be around, and he often created funny games with his imagination for us to play. Once we were on our way to the beach and having been convinced that someone had stolen our Fairy liquid, and having happened to spot a bottle in someone else's tent, tried to convince me, yes an 8 year old, to go and take it back. To my knowledge I don't think I did, and fortunately I think he was joking. I don't think it would have gone down too well but it was so funny at the time.

Later on my parents, Kim and I went on a few summer holidays to Turkey. Every night Dad would insist on wearing his 'Noah's Ark' waistcoat out to dinner (to mine and Kim's horror!) which the locals absolutely loved. When Kim and I would moan about him wearing the waistcoat he would proudly proclaim 'Look…at least I'm not wearing socks and sandals!' Even on holiday dad took every opportunity to share the gospel with people, and the people there really loved him, and responded to him. Some of the locals started calling my parents their 'English mum and dad'.

Growing up with your dad as a vicar, you see the side of him that others don't often see. To me he was just my dad. He was funny and silly and sometimes got cross with me!

My dad is so special to me and I'm so very proud of the way he shares the whole truth of the gospel without fear, he truly does inspire me every day. I can honestly say that I wouldn't have wanted my childhood to have been anything else.

Dad has built up an awesome congregation at Christchurch, and they too have that same integrity, passion and love that he shows everyday. Christchurch has been my home church for nearly 20 years. I've grown up there and so when dad leaves it will be really hard for all of us. People may not realize this but when dad gets hurt, attacked or targeted then it affects the whole family. I know that mum and dad protected us from much of the troubles that came their way and this couldn't have been easy. For all the difficult times there have definitely been more happy times. As a family we've had some great experiences and met some great people who have supported Dad and his ministry. I know they will always be special to us and always be a part of our family too. I'm so thankful and grateful for all my Dad is and all he will yet become. I'm so blessed to have him as my dad.

**Chapter Eight:**

## WHAT DOES THE FUTURE HOLD?
### (2009 - ?)

I told you that Charm and the family would be honest! Some of the things that our children wrote upset Charm and I a lot. They kept a lot from us and their stories reflect the enormous cost of being a vicar. Being a vicar people think that they own your time twenty four hours a day and it's easy to fall into that trap. The result is that there's a cost on your family and we are truly sorry wherever any of our children felt that we didn't give them enough time.

In January 2009 I went to my doctor. He had been a great help to me over the years and I valued his comments. After some discussion we came to an agreement that I had had enough. I was worn out. He agreed to submit his medical opinion about my condition to the Church of England and our Bishop also submitted his report stating that I needed to retire on health grounds. For someone who had been so full of energy this was hard, but in my heart I knew it was right. The Pensions Board accepted their reports and I contacted the Bishop, giving my resignation. My final services were to be on July 12th 2009.

It's difficult to put into words how I feel. Part of me will be incredibly sad to go after nearly twenty years but another part knows that this is the right time. We have some great and lasting memories of our time from pantomimes to drains and everything in between! There were many occasions when I had to ask Paul to come and help me with the vicarage drains using the rods and getting plastered as the blockage suddenly broke! It was only years later that I realised I could have rung the diocese for help! I believe that I have finished what I was called to do here.

I thought it could be done in less time but I was wrong! I look at the vision banner and I look at the people and I thank God for what He's done and is doing. I have taught over a hundred teaching series to try to enable people to deepen their walk with God, with one another, and to have God's heart for those who don't yet know Him. Now the church needs God's new leader to enable the vision to go forward. Is letting go hard? I honestly have to say No! Two or three years ago it would have been but not now. I really do feel spent! Some hard years in the ministry have definitely taken their toll.

The final services will be difficult as it's the end of an era and we shall miss the people. I'd like to speak to the church family in the morning to encourage them to keep on keeping on! I'm hoping that we can get something in the local paper nearer the time so that anyone we've had contact with over the years can come along in the evening. And then that will be it!

Charm and I will be moving to our new home which is called Mulligans. This is a golfing term meaning another chance! That's very apt for us. On the doormat inside it says, "Casi Cielo," which means "Nearly Heaven." Charm and I are so thrilled to have our own home at long last! We haven't had our own home to live in for nearly thirty years and so we appreciate it so much. After living so long on council estates we will now be looking out at fields and horses and woods! We shall be growing our own vegetables and keeping hens! I shall play some golf and walk a lot with the dogs! Will I be slipping into obscurity then? No!

I shall be continuing my work with Worcester Warriors, continuing to write, and I hope to get involved in the local community. I also hope to do some teaching at conferences etc. both here and abroad. I have such a great desire to share the Gospel with people and to enable Christians to know that they are not holding the fort until Jesus comes back but they're

Kingdom people with a mission! If all Jesus came to do was to save people then He'd have taken us straight to Heaven the moment we received Him. The fact is that a Christian is called to be salt and light and to make a difference in this world. In spite of the mess the world is in there's still hope because I believe with all my heart that Jesus can change people and situations. I've seen this happen time and time again and always for the good.

I believe that there's a battle for truth today. Sadly all the recent furore amongst our MPs has highlighted what happens when a nation turns its back on God and His laws. Our leaders no longer feel guilty about lies and deception. The world would tell us that it doesn't matter what you believe so long as you are sincere but what if you are sincerely wrong! Jesus said:- "I am the Way, the Truth and the Life." (John's Gospel Chapter 14 verse 6.) People say that Jesus was a good man with some wonderful teaching but stating that He was THE TRUTH makes Jesus very non-politically correct! No one else said the things He said and no one else did the things He did, so that definitely puts Him in a different category to others. Is there a Truth that is not at the mercy of time, culture and opinion and is forever True no matter what we feel or think? Absolutely! And it's found in the person of Jesus.

Most people have no idea of who Jesus is and what He can do in a person. I have battled hard all my life against religion because it clouds the issue. Religion is full of rules and regulations and it's man-made. So many people are put off Jesus because of this. The fact is that he didn't come to bring a whole bunch of rules. He came to bring us life, to offer us a fresh start, and a living relationship with God day by day. One of the best illustrations that shows the difference between Christianity and other religions is DO versus DONE. Religion is all about doing things to try to please God whereas

Christianity is all about what Jesus has done for us on the Cross to deal with our sin. Writing those two words on a slip of paper reminds people about what sets Christianity apart.

As far as I'm concerned every day is a new day of grace. I don't have to be weighed down by yesterday's failures or worry about tomorrow. I just thank God for his presence and I ask to journey with Him. I remind myself that because of His grace I am a Kingdom person and so I ask Him to enable me to touch other lives and situations with His love and truth. Jesus believed in people. He saw the hidden potential to be a Kingdom person. He saw beyond the flaws and failures to who they could become if God's love and power were released in their lives. And so I ask Him to help me to see people as He sees them. The world sees a person as made up of body and soul whereas God created us with a spirit too which is what connects us to Him. The book of Ecclesiastes says that God has "Set eternity in the hearts of men" (Chapter 3 verse 11). There is a longing deep in people's hearts that nothing in this world can fulfil until their spirit comes alive to God. That is the problem with secular counseling. It's only dealing with the body and the soul. So many of our problems lie in our spirit and until that is healed we will not know true freedom. I want to continue to enable people to realise who they were created to be. I really can't think of anything greater and so that's what I'll be doing until my journey ends!

If you've read this far I do so hope that you've been encouraged and challenged.

Thank you for joining me on my journey. As you now realise, it has been quite unusual! The fact is though that everyone has a story and I like listening to other people's stories. Sometimes I'm asked about my story and to stop the person being bored I've distilled it in under a hundred words! This is my story: "I came from a broken home and didn't feel loved. I looked for love but it always had strings attached and I got badly hurt. So I put up barriers and put on masks and I was a mess inside. Then someone cared enough to introduce me to Jesus and I began to feel hope. Slowly the barriers came down and the masks came off as I realised that I was loved unconditionally. Nearly forty years on He's still working on me but I'm not who I was. The fear and loneliness and pretence have gone." So there you have it!

I'm eternally grateful to God for bringing Charm into my life. Her love and support have been priceless over the years and our love keeps growing. We recently celebrated my brother's Ruby Wedding Anniversary and lots of the family were there, which reminded me how vital family is. God willing, Charm and I will be celebrating our forty years together very soon and it too will be a great family occasion!

As you've gathered by now I'm quite a maverick! I've been called it at various times and it also applies to my golf! When my friend Ian and I had some lessons the pro would try and teach us to play safe but it never worked. We play over the trees, under the trees, through the trees, or remove the trees and it usually works well! Playing safe is not my style.

If there are any issues raised that you'd like to discuss then you can contact me through ~~Christist Church.~~ *my web*

rs (or are

124